# CITING ATHEISTS

# Citing Atheists

### Quotes of Agnosticism, Non-Theism, Skepticism, Irreligion, Free Thought, and Philosophy

## By Steve Dustcircle

http://www.alifebeyondbooks.com

aLife Beyond Books
c/o Hudson Media
P.O. Box 163381
Columbus, Ohio 43216
www.alifebeyondbooks.com

Ordering Information:

Quantity sales. Special discounts are available on quantity purchases by corporations, associations, and others. For details, contact the publisher at the address above.

Printed in the United States of America

Publisher's Cataloging-in-Publication data
Dustcircle, Steve.
Citing Atheists : Quotes of Agnosticism, Non-Theism, Skepticism, Irreligion, Free Thought, and Philosophy / Steve Dustcircle.
p. cm.

ISBN-13: 978-1507733813 (amazon)
ISBN-10: 150773381X (amazon)

1. Reference 2. Atheism 3. Non-Fiction

First Edition

10 9 8 7 6 5 4 3 2 1

# Citing Atheists

# CONTENTS:

# Introduction:

I want to thank everyone who has fed me knowledge and wisdom over the years, either directly and personally, or unknowingly through their writings or podcasts.

Many of these quotes come from books I have read, websites I visit, and newsletters I receive. Mostly, I am deeply indebted to the Freedom from Religion Foundation (http://www.FFRF.org) for their hard work putting together their daily *Freethought of the Day*, from which I have acquired at least half of these quotes.

However, there are not atheist quotes in this book. There are also a few that lean political in a secular manner. There are also some quotes on science and philosophy. Finally, there are even a few quotes by religious people, ones that I feel are appalling.

This quote book is in alphabetical order by the person's last name (or by their popular name, as in Plato, Cicero or Augustine). The *Table of Contents* are simply a jump-to option, the name of the "chapter" being random—whoever happens to be at the top of the page.

I don't claim that this slim volume is definitive. On the contrary. I feel that these quotes spoke most to me, coming from a religious background and moving into a future of skepticism and free thought. Will there be a *sequel* to this volume (or a deluxe edition)? I sure do hope so.

While there are several, thick volumes of quote books out there, many of them being called definitive, I feel that I am providing a comprehensive, condensed volume here—almost a *best of.*

Other volumes I would highly recommend are:

- *2000 Years of Disbelief* – James A. Haugt
- *The Atheist's Bible* – Joan Konner
- *The Big Book of Quotations for Atheists* – I. M. Probulos
- *Blasphemy* – Jon Webster
- *The Quotable Atheist* – Jack Huberman
- *The Portable Atheist* – Christopher Hitchens

Thank you for buying this book, and I hope you check out some of my other books, including the political/rights quote book, *The Quotable Dissenting Heretic.*

– Steve Dustcircle, Editor

# ABBOT

That great and growing evils render it a paramount patriotic duty on the part of American citizens, who comprehend the priceless value of pure Secular government, to take active measures for the immediate and absolute secularization of the state, and we earnestly urge them to organize without delay for this purpose.

- Francis Ellingwood Abbot

[Religions] impose antiquated and narrow beliefs which are entirely unsuitable for a being who knows nothing and can affirm nothing.

- Louise Victorine Ackermann

If you describe yourself as 'Atheist,' some people will say, 'Don't you mean "Agnostic"?' ' I have to reply that I really *do* mean Atheist. I really do not believe that there is a god—in fact I am convinced that there is not a god (a subtle difference). I see not a shred of evidence to suggest that there is one. It's easier to say that I am a radical Atheist, just to signal that I really mean it, have thought about it a great deal, and that it's an opinion I hold seriously. It's funny how many people are genuinely surprised to hear a view expressed so strongly. In England we seem to have drifted from vague wishy-washy Anglicanism to vague wishy-washy Agnosticism—both of which I think betoken a desire not to have to think about things too much.

- Douglas Adams

Now, the invention of the scientific method is, I'm sure we'll all agree, the most powerful intellectual idea, the most powerful framework for thinking and investigating and understanding and challenging the world around us that there is, and it rests on the premise that any idea is there to be attacked. If it withstands the attack then it lives to fight another day and if it doesn't withstand the attack then down it goes. Religion doesn't seem to work like that. It has certain ideas at the heart of it which we call sacred or holy or whatever.

- Douglas Adams

Can a free government possibly exist with the Roman Catholic religion?

- John Adams

Have you considered that system of holy lies and pious frauds that has raged and triumphed for 1,500 years?

- John Adams

People are not disposed to inquire for piety, integrity, good sense or learning in a young preacher, but for stupidity (for so I must call the pretended sanctity of some absolute dunces), irresistible grace, and original sin.

- John Adams

The Government of the United States of America is not in any sense founded on the Christian religion.

- John Adams

This would be the best of all possible worlds, if there were no religion in it.

- John Adams

Twenty times in the course of my late readings, I have been on the point of breaking out, 'This would be the best of all worlds if there were no religion in it!'

- John Adams

Until this awful blasphemy [the Incarnation] is got rid of, there never will be any liberal science in the world.

- John Adams

A wise man has told us that 'men are once for all so made that they prefer a rational world to believe in and live in' .

- Jane Addams

The very word woman in the writings of the church fathers stood for the basest temptations.

- Jane Addams

For more than three thousand years men have quarreled concerning the formulas of their faith. The earth has been drenched with blood shed in this cause, the face of day darkened with the blackness of the crimes perpetrated in its name. There have been no dirtier wars than religious wars, no bitterer hates than religious hates, no fiendish cruelty like religious cruelty; no baser baseness than religious baseness. It has destroyed the peace of families, turned the father against the son, the brother against the brother. And for what? Are we any nearer to unanimity? On the contrary, diversity within the churches and without has never been so widespread as at present. Sects and factions are multiplying on every hand, and every new schism is but the parent of a dozen others.

- Felix Adler

We propose entirely to exclude prayer and every form of ritual . . . to occupy that common ground where we may all meet, believers and unbelievers . . . be one with us where there is nothing to divide, in action. Diversity in creed, unanimity in the deed.

- Felix Adler

As regards the individual nature, woman is defective and misbegotten, for the active force in the male seed tends to the production of a perfect likeness in the masculine sex; while the production of woman comes from a defect in the active force or from some material indisposition, or even from some external influence.

- Thomas Aguinas

It is a principle innate and co-natural to every man to have an insatiable inclination to the truth, and to seek for it as for hid treasure. . . .

- Thomas Aikenhead

[Calvinism is] a doctrine derogatory to the nature of man and the rank and character of being which he holds in the universe. . . .

- Ethan Allen

I believe it is the imposition of a dictatorship that increasing numbers on the Christian Right now wish to construct in the United States. . . . They believe that Christianity should be the official religion of the United States and that American laws should be specifically Christian.

-Steve Allen

It was only when I finally undertook to read the Bible through from beginning to end that I perceived that its depiction of the Lord God—whom I had always viewed as the very embodiment of perfection—was actually that of a monstrous, vengeful tyrant, far exceeding in bloodthirstiness and insane savagery the depredations of Hitler, Stalin, Pol Pot, Attila the Hun, or any other mass murderer of ancient or modern history.

- Steve Allen

How can I believe in God when just last week I got my tongue caught in the roller of an electric typewriter?

- Woody Allen

I am a Jew only in the sense that I was born into a Jewish family. I have no interest in the organized religions beyond a certain cerebral historical curiosity. They are all nonsense to me in their basic premises. . . . I'm agnostic, but I have one foot in atheism.

- Woody Allen

Not only is there no God, but try getting a plumber on weekends.

- Woody Allen

To you, I'm an atheist. To God, I'm the loyal opposition.

- Woody Allen

He who is not angry when there is just cause for anger is immoral. Why? Because anger looks to the good of justice. And if you can live amid injustice without anger, you are immoral as well as unjust.

- St. Thomas Aquinas

I am an atheist, I have no religious beliefs. And obviously I don't believe in spirituality of some kind.

- Javed Akhtar

Nothing is more dangerous than an idea, when a man has only one idea.

- Alaine

I'm an atheist, . . . You could say that I'm agnostic, but that's just a certain kind of atheist. If I were a gambling man I would put all my money on there not being anything other than this universe.

- Steve Albini

People use God to fill in the spaces in the gaps of their knowledge. . . . As we follow the trajectory of knowledge, the need for a God just dwindles, and it approaches zero.

- Steve Albini

I asked myself: Why should I burn in hell just because I'm drinking this? But what prompted me even more was the fact that the killers of 9/11 all believed in the same God I believed in.

- Ayaan Hirsi Ali

I had left God behind years ago. I was an atheist. . . . From now on I could step firmly on the ground that was under my feet and navigate based on my own reason and self-respect. My moral compass was within myself, not in the pages of a sacred book. . . . All life is problem solving. . . . There are no absolutes; progress comes through critical thought. . . . Reason, not obedience, should guide our lives. Though it took centuries to crumble, the entire ossified cage of European social hierarchy—from kings to serfs, and between men and women, all of it shored up by the Catholic Church—was destroyed by this thought.

- Ayaan Hirsi Ali

How often in our house had I heard talk of superstitious idiots, often relatives, who hated a Satan they never knew and worshiped a God they didn't have the brains to doubt?

- Tariq Ali

I grew up an atheist. I make no secret of it. It was acceptable. In fact, when I think back, none of my friends were believers. None of them were religious; maybe a few were believers. But very few were religious in temperament.

- Tariq Ali

We grew up in Lahore, which had been one of the most cosmopolitan towns in India. Then you had the partition of India, and you had massive killings. This is not much talked about these days, but nearly two million people died, as Hindus, Muslims, and Sikhs slaughtered each other to create this state . . . when you realized what had happened, how much killing had gone on, you did ask yourself, 'Was it worth it?'

- Tariq Ali

If you think you've got an inside track to absolute truth, you become doctrinaire, humorless and intellectually constipated. The greatest crimes in history have been perpetrated by such religious and political and racial fanatics.

- Saul Alinsky

In those parts of the world where learning and science have prevailed, miracles have ceased.

- Ethan Allen

The vast mass of existing gods or divine persons, when we come to analyze them, do actually turn out to be dead and deified

18

human beings. . . . I believe corpse worship is the protoplasm of religion.

- Grant Allen

Are we really that special? I don't think so.

- William Anders

I'm an Atheist. I don't believe in God, Gods, Godlets or any sort of higher power beyond the universe itself, which seems quite high and powerful enough to me. I don't believe in life after death, channeling chat rooms with the dead, reincarnation, telekinesis or any miracles but the miracle of life and consciousness, which again strike me as miracles in nearly obscene abundance. . . . I'm convinced that the world as we see it was shaped by the again genuinely miraculous, let's even say transcendent, hand of evolution through natural selection.

- Natalie Angier

Reason, which we recognize as our highest and only law-giver, commands us to be free.

- Mathilde Franziska Giesler Anneke

Ethical people will do what is right, no matter what they are told. Religious people will do what they are told, no matter what is right.

- Anonymous

I distrust those people who know so well what God wants them to do because I notice it always coincides with their own desires.

- Susan B. Anthony

I never accepted religion so I had nothing to reject as such. The history of 'Christinsanity' (my own coinage of which I am proud!) is so brutal of mind, emotions, freedom, progress, science and all that I hold precious, tat by any standards of justice its leaders in almost any given period would be incarcerated for life, or worse!

- Madison Arnold

It is almost impossible to exaggerate the proneness of the human mind to take miracles as evidence, and to seek for miracles as evidence.

- Matthew Arnold

Rigorous teachers seized my youth

And purged its faith, and trimm'd its fire

Show'd me the high, white star of Truth.

- Matthew Arnold

The personages of the Christian heaven and their conversations are no more matter of fact than the personages of the Greek Olympus and their conversations.

- Matthew Arnold

I am Jewish in the sense that if an Arab wanted to throw a rock at a Jew, I would qualify as a target as far as he was concerned. However, I do not practice Judaism or any other religion.

- Isaac Asimov

I am prejudiced against religion because I know the history of religion, and it is the history of human misery and of black crimes.

- Isaac Asimov

I must say that I stand amazed at the highly intelligent people who have taken so much of the Bible so seriously

- Isaac Asimov

It is an excellent sign that the right wing is trembling before a few thousand Humanists. We are weak and yet feared. Let's give them more cause to fear!

- Isaac Asimov

I want to be a human being, nothing more and nothing less.

- Isaac Asimov

I would not be satisfied to have my kids choose to be religious without trying to argue them out of it, just as I would not be satisfied to have them decide to smoke regularly or engage in any other practice I considered detrimental to mind or body.

- Isaac Asimov

Just the force of rational argument in the end cannot be withstood.

- Isaac Asimov

Nobody but a dedicated Christian could possibly read the gospels and not see them as a tissue of nonsense.

- Isaac Asimov

Properly read, the Bible is the most potent force for atheism ever conceived.

- Isaac Asimov

To those who are trained in science, creationism seems like a bad dream, a sudden coming back to life of a nightmare, a renewed march of an Army of the Night risen to challenge free thought and enlightenment.

- Isaac Asimov

If I were not an atheist, I would believe in a God who would choose to save people on the basis of the totality of their lives and not the pattern of their words. I think he would prefer an honest and righteous atheist to a TV preacher whose every word is God, God, God, and whose every deed is foul, foul, foul.

- Isaac Asimov

I'm an agnostic.

- David Attenborough

It never really occurred to me to believe in God. And I had nothing to rebel against. My parents told me nothing whatsoever. But I do remember looks at y headmaster delivering a sermon, a classicist, extremely clever . . . and thinking, he can't really believe all that, can he? How incredible!

- David Attenborough

A doctrinaire agnostic is different from someone who doesn't know what they believe. A doctrinaire agnostic believes quite passionately that there are certain things that you cannot know, and therefore ought not to make pronouncements about. In other words, the only things you can call knowledge are things that can be scientifically tested.

- Margaret Atwood

I was reading the Bible—some of us still do that, you know—and I saw the tale of Jacob and his wives and handmaids, a kind of early Baby M. This is not an attack on Christianity, but the fact is Christians have long persecuted other sects and each other, as they are in Northern Ireland today. People were saying things like, 'A woman's place is in the home.' And I got to thinking, well, how would someone enforce thoughts like that?

- Margaret Atwood

Woman does not possess the image of God in herself but only when taken together with the male who is her head, so that the whole substance is one image. But when she is assigned the role as helpmate, a function that pertains to her alone, then she is not the image of God. But as far as the man is concerned, he is by himself alone the image of God just as fully and completely as when he and the woman are joined together into one.

- Augustine

While some pre-Christian groups outlawed slavery, Christianity continued it and expanded it worldwide. There were probably far more people enslaved (tens if millions) under Christian empires than in all pre-Christian empires combined.

- Hector Avalos

I do not believe in God. It seems to me that theists of all kinds have very largely failed to make their concept of a deity intelligible; and to the extent that they have made it intelligible, they have given us no reason to think that anything answers to it.

- Alfred Jules Ayer

My recent experiences have slightly weakened my conviction that my genuine death, which is due fairly soon, will be the end of me, though I continue to hope that it will be. They have not weakened my conviction that there is no god. I trust that my remaining an atheist will allay the anxieties of my fellow supporters of the British Humanist Association, the Rationalist Press Association and the South Place Ethical Society.

- Alfred Jules Ayer

# BACHELET

I'm agnostic. . . . I believe in the state.

- Michelle Bachelet

I was a woman, a divorcée, a socialist, an agnostic . . . all possible sins together.

- Michelle Bachelet

For what a man had rather were true he more readily believes.

- Francis Bacon

Great and terrible systems of divinity and philosophy lie round about us, which, if true, might drive a wise man mad.

- Walter Bagehot

The secular equivalent of faith in God . . . is faith in the human community and its evolving procedures.

- Annette Baier

All religions, with their gods, their demigods, and their prophets, their messiahs and their saints, were created by the credulous fancy of men who had not attained the full development and full possession of their faculties.

- Mikhail Bakunin

Freedom, morality, and the human dignity of the individual consists precisely in this; that he does good not because he is forced to do so, but because he freely conceives it, wants it, and loves it.

- Mikhail Bakunin

[Jehovah is] certainly the most jealous, the most vain, the most ferocious, the most unjust, the most bloodthirsty, the most despotic, and the most hostile to human dignity and liberty.

- Mikhail Bakunin

On behalf of human liberty, dignity and prosperity, we believe it our duty to recover from heaven the goods which it has stolen and return them to earth. If God is, man is a slave; now, man can and must be free; then, God does not exist. A jealous lover of human liberty, and deeming it the absolute condition of all that we admire and respect in humanity, I reverse the phrase of Voltaire, and say that, if God really existed, it would be necessary to abolish him.

- Mikhail Bakunin

If the concept of God has any validity or use, it can only be to make us larger, freer, and more loving. If God cannot do this, then it is time we got rid of him.

- James Baldwin

I always say, 'I don't believe in God, I believe in Al Pacino'—and that's true.

- Javier Bardem

I wasn't a very committed Catholic before, but when that happened it suddenly all felt so obvious: I now believe religion is our attempt to find an explanation; to feel more protected.

- Javier Bardem

I threw out the bath water, and there was no baby there.

- Dan Barker

The United States of America is not in any sense founded on the Christian religion.

- Joel Barlow

Isn't believing in God like wearing chain mail? . . . In that you just don't do it anymore.

- Paul Barman

If the ignorance of nature gave birth to the gods, knowledge of nature is destined to destroy them.

- Baron d'Holbach

In all parts of our globe, fanatics have cut each other's throats, publicly burnt each other, committed without a scruple and even as a duty, the greatest crimes, and shed torrents of blood. . . . Savage and furious nations, perpetually at war, adore, under divers names, some God, conformable to their ideas, that is to say, cruel, carnivorous, selfish, blood-thirsty. We find, in all the religions, 'a God of armies,' a 'jealous God,' an 'avenging God,' a 'destroying God,' a 'God,' who is pleased with carnage, and whom his worshipers consider it a duty to serve. Lambs, bulls, children, men, and women, are sacrificed to him. Zealous servants of this barbarous God think themselves obliged even to offer up themselves as a sacrifice to him. Madmen may everywhere be seen, who, after meditating upon their terrible God, imagine that to please him they must inflict on themselves, the most exquisite torments. The gloomy ideas formed of the deity, far from consoling them, have every where disquieted their minds, and prejudiced follies destructive to happiness. How could the human mind progress, while tormented with frightful phantoms, and guided by men, interested in perpetuating its ignorance and fears? Man has been forced to vegetate in his primitive stupidity: he has been taught stories about invisible powers upon whom his happiness was supposed to depend. Occupied solely by his fears, and by unintelligible reveries, he has always been at the mercy of priests, who have reserved to themselves the right of thinking for him, and of directing his actions.

- Baron d'Holbach

Knowledge, Reason, and Liberty, can alone reform and make men happier.

- Baron d'Holbach

Religion is a mere castle in the air. Theology is ignorance of natural causes; a tissue of fallacies and contradictions.

- Baron d'Holbach

Emancipate thy mind from the idle fears of Superstition and the wicked arts of priesthood.

- John Baskerville

God is the only being who does not have to exist in order to reign.

- Charles Baudelaire

It is pure illusion to think that an opinion which passes down from century to century to century, from generation to generation, may not be entirely false.

- Pierre Bayle

No nations are more warlike than those which profess Christianity.

- Pierre Bayle

Christianity is the enemy of liberty and civilization. It has kept mankind in slavery and oppression. The Church and the State have always fraternally united to exploit the people.

- August Bebel

I'm pathetically pragmatic. . . . I don't believe that there's a higher power that created human beings.

- Joy Behar

I'm sustained by my family, my life, my brain. But I don't believe there's an afterlife.

- Joy Behar

I never gave her [my daughter] any religion, because I felt that I was brainwashed. . . . This is what I didn't want my daughter to have. So that's why I didn't want her to go to Catholic school or learn any of that.

- Joy Behar

I was on track to eternal Mormon stardom, reserved especially for faithful men in a church run by men.

- Steve Benson

We must never retreat in the face of threats or punishments dispensed by theocratic terrorists more interested in protecting their power and indulging their vanity, than in advancing the human condition. If, as the true believers claim, the word 'gospel' means good news, then the good news for me is that there is no gospel, other than what I can define for myself, by observation and conscience. As a freethinking human being, I have come not to favor or fear religion, but to face and fight it as an impediment to civilized advancement.

- Steve Benson

No power of government ought to be employed in the endeavor to establish any system or article of belief on the subject of religion. . . . In no instance has a system in regard to religion been ever established, but for the purpose, as well as with the effect of its being made an instrument of intimidation, corruption, and delusion, for the support of depredation and oppression in the hands of the governments.

- Jeremy Bentham

Man is a solitary sorting machine.

- Henri Bergson

I believe nothing.

- Hector Berlioz

I am . . . culturally Catholic, but spiritually agnostic.

- Gael Garcia Bernal

To kill a pagan is to win glory for it gives glory to Christ.

- St. Bernard of Clairvaux

[Roy Torcaso] was an activist to the end of his life. He just did not believe that religion should enforce its views on the whole of society. He really believed that everyone should have the right to choose their own views.

- Linda Bernstein

I rejoice that I played my part in that educating of England which has made impossible for evermore the crude superstitions of the past, and the repetition of the cruelties and injustices under which preceding heretics suffered.

- Annie Besant

Prayer belongs in churches and in homes. It does not belong in government meetings. Perhaps the Christians will show a little charity to those of us who don't agree with their views and separate their beliefs from the government business at hand.

- Roy Birk

I have always read the ancient pagans with infinite pleasure, while in Christian writers I find only system, egoism, intolerance, and a complete lack of artistic taste.

- Georges Bizet

Religion is a means of exploitation employed by the strong against the weak; religion is a cloak of ambition, injustice and vice. . . . Truth breaks free, science is popularized, and religion totters; soon it will fall, in the course of centuries—that is, tomorrow. . . . In good time we shall only have to deal with reason.

- Georges Bizet

I do not believe in religion, but if I had to choose one, it would be Buddhism.

- Björk

I've got my own religion. Iceland sets a world-record. The United Nations asked people from all over the world a series of questions. Iceland stuck out on one thing. When we were asked what do we believe, 90% said, 'ourselves.' I think I'm in that group. If I get into trouble, there's no God or Allah to sort me out. I have to do it myself.

- Björk

[It] was largely to escape religious test oaths and declarations that a great many of the early colonists left Europe and came here hoping to worship in their own way. It soon developed, however, that many of those who had fled to escape religious test oaths turned out to be perfectly willing, when they had the power to do so, to force dissenters from their faith to take test oaths in conformity with the faith. . . . There were, however, wise and farseeing men in the Colonies—too many to mention—who spoke out against test oaths and all the philosophy of intolerance behind them. . . . We repeat and again reaffirm that neither a State nor the Federal Government can constitutionally force a person 'to profess a belief or disbelief in any religion.' Neither can constitutionally pass laws or impose requirements which aid all religions as against nonbelievers, and neither can aid those religions based on a belief in the existence of God as against those religions founded on different beliefs.

- Hugo Black

When the power, prestige and financial support of government is placed behind a particular religious belief, the indirect coercive pressure upon religious minorities to conform to the prevailing officially approved religion is plain.

- Hugo Black

Every denial of education, every refusal of advantages to women, may be traced to this dogma [of original sin], which first began to spread its baleful influence with the rise of the power of the priesthood and the corruption of the early Church.

- Lillie Devereux Blake

Prisons are built with stones of Law, Brothels with bricks of Religion.

- William Blake

I have a firm belief in such things as, you know, the water, the Earth, the trees and sky. And I'm wondering, it is increasingly difficult to find those elements in nature, because it's nature I believe in rather than some spiritual thing. . . . And I do suppose that science has taken, to a large extent and for a number of people, has taken the place of religion . . . that one can have more belief in scientific miracles than you do in God miracles. It's inevitable that we will eventually diffuse into nothingness.

- Bill Blass

I cannot believe that any religion has been revealed to Man by God. Because a revealed religion would be perfect, but no known religion is perfect; and because history and science show us that known religions have not been revealed but have been evolved from other traditions.

- Robert Blatchford

My faith is in mankind and the marvels accomplished by human ingenuity and drive.

- Robyn Blumner

Reason has been under siege and been slapped around. Believing things on the basis of something other than evidence and reason causes people to misconstrue what's good for them.

- Peter Boghossian

Religious wars are basically people killing each other over who has the better imaginary friend.

- Napolean Bonararte

Our humanist attitude should therefore throughout be to stress what we all have in common with each other and relegate quarrelsome religion to the private domain where it can do [less] harm.

- Hermann Bondi

Though I make this concession as to my body, my philosophical belief remains unaltered.

- Rosa Bonheur

The Catholic Church teaches that faith is a gift from God, and it's a gift I never received apparently. It always seemed kind of strange to me that we're depending on this supernatural power and there's no real evidence that it exists.

- Ben Bova

The difference between science and most religions is that science admits that we don't know everything.

- Ben Bova

When I started understanding how science works, it occurred to me that there just is no evidence that there is a God.

- Ben Bova

Why burn? The answer is simple. Read the Bible—the Koran—the theologians and philosophers of the world.

- Meg Bowman

Belief in God and in a Hereafter dropped considerably as the level of scientific achievement increased.

- Paul D. Boyer

I wonder if in the United States we will ever reach the day when the man-made concept of a God will not appear on our money, and for political survival must be invoked by those who seek to represent us in our democracy.

- Paul D. Boyer

My views have changed from a belief that my prayers were heard to clear atheism. . . . Over and over, expanding scientific knowledge has shown religious claims to be false. None of the beliefs in gods has any merit.

- Paul D. Boyer

Atheism, properly understood, is no mere disbelief; is in no wise a cold, barren negative; it is, on the contrary, a hearty, fruitful affirmation of all truth, and involves the positive assertion of action of highest humanity.

- Charles Bradlaugh

I maintain that thoughtful Atheism affords greater possibility for human happiness than any system yet based on, or possible to be founded on, Theism, and that the lives of true Atheists must be more virtuous—because more human—than those of the believers in Deity

- Charles Bradlaugh

The lives of atheists must be more virtuous—because more human—than those of the believers in Deity.

- Charles Bradlaugh

Away with all these gods and godlings; they are worse than useless.

- Hypatia Bradlaugh

The only true immortality lies in one's children.

- Johannes Brahms

I will not swear on God. I will not swear on God, because I don't believe in the conceptual sense and in this nonsense. What I will swear on is my children and my grandchildren.

- Marlon Brando

Everything that is doddering, squint-eyed, vile, polluted and grotesque is summoned up for me in that one word: God!

- Andre Breton

[Religion is] nothing more than a type of submission to authority.

- Paul Broca

Only Puritans think of the Devil as the most fascinating figure in the universe.

- Heywood C. Broun

If anyone in this audience believes that God made his body, and your body is dirty, the fault lies with the manufacturer.

- Lenny Bruce

[Before *Force and Matter*, 1855] what did the world at large know then of the first achievements of science? The vast majority were sunk in their blind faith in authority and the Bible . . . they did not wish to know, because such things clearly contradicted the pleasant legends of the Bible, whose naive story of creation led to little reflection. Into this frog-pond was suddenly flung the log of *Force and Matter*. No wonder there was a universal croak.

- Alexander Buchner

First you adduce morality as a proof of God, and then cite God in support of morality. You reason in a beautiful circle, like a dog biting his own tail.

- Georg Buchner

There is no God. . . . God cannot have created the world.

- Georg Buchner

According to the unanimous testimony of traders, philosophers, navigators and missionaries, there exists a by no means small number of peoples, who have either no trace of religious belief, or who have it in so strange and imperfect a form that it scarcely deserves the name of religion. If there are, therefore, many philosophers and naturalists who look to 'religiosity,' and more particularly to the idea of God as the distinctive feature of humanity, the contention referred to must either be false, or we must make up our own minds to deny human character to by no means a small number of actual and undoubted specimens of mankind.

- Ludwig Buchner

I feel no need for any other faith than my faith in human beings. Like Confucius of old, I am so absorbed in the wonder of earth and the life upon it that I cannot think of heaven and the angels.

- Pearl S. Buck

It may be that religion is dead, and if it is, we had better know it and set ourselves to try to discover other sources of moral strength before it is too late.

- Pearl S. Buck

Agnosticism, once defiant, had gone underground. I no longer had the desire to nail my theses to his church door. By now I knew we didn't have much time left, and I didn't want to spend it locking theological horns.

- Christopher Buckley

I'm no longer a believer, but I haven't quite reached the point of reading aloud from Christopher Hitchens' 'God Is Not Great' at deathbeds of loved ones.

- Christopher Buckley

Believe not because some old manuscripts are produced, believe not because it is your national belief, believe not because you have been made to believe from your childhood, but reason truth out; and after you have analyzed it, then if you find it will do good to one and all; believe it, live up to it and help others live up to it.

- Buddha

Thank God, I'm still an atheist.

- Luis Bunuel

And to think of this great country in danger of being dominated by people ignorant enough to take a few ancient Babylonian legends as the canons of modern culture. Our scientific men are paying for their failure to speak out earlier. There is no use now talking evolution to these people. Their ears are stuffed with

Genesis.

- Luther Burbank

As a scientist, I can not help feeling that all religions are on a tottering foundation. None is perfect or inspired. The idea that a good God would send people to a burning hell is utterly damnable to me. I don't want to have anything to do with such a God. I am an infidel today.

- Luther Burbank

Children are the greatest sufferers from outgrown theologies.

- Luther Burbank

Jesus wasn't the messiah. Get back, I'm a heretic and I'm on fire.

- Bo Burnham

It becomes a man of sense to think for himself; particularly in a case where all men are equally interested, and where, indeed, all men are equally in the dark.

- Robert Burns

Men who had not progressed as far as we have tried to interpret [evolution] some two thousand years ago. It is not strange that they made mistakes. They were ignorant and superstitious.

- Edgar Rice Burroughs

The deeper our insight into the methods of nature . . . the more incredible the popular Christianity seems to us.

- John Burroughs

The more I study religions the more I am convinced that man never worshiped anyone but himself.

- Richard Burton

Prayers are to men as dolls are to children. They are not without use and comfort, but it is not easy to take them very seriously.

- Samuel Butler

Because of [Hugh Everett's] loudly avowed atheism, he was labeled 'the heretic' by devout classmates.

- Peter Byrne

# CALVIN

Thus the woman, who had perversely exceeded her proper bounds, is forced back to her own position. She had, indeed, previously been subject to her husband, but that was a liberal and gentle subjection; now, however, she is cast into servitude.

- John Calvin

I've sworn off agnosticism, which I now call cowardly atheism. I've come to the position that in the complete absence of any supporting data whatsoever for the persistence of the individual in some spiritual form, it is necessary to operate under the provisional conclusion that there is no afterlife and then be ready to amend that if I find out otherwise.

- James Cameron

No wonder their 'flocks' are 'low in education.'

- Emily Cape

What would Christ do about syphilis? Well, what should he do? Christ, being possessed of miraculous powers, why does he not obliterate syphilis from the face of the earth? Does *Spirochaeta pallida*, the organism causing syphilis, perform any useful function in the economy of nature? If not, why not obliterate it? Who is better equipped to do this than Jesus Christ?

- Ira Cardiff

The fable of a god or gods visiting the earth did not originate with Christianity.

- Richard Carlile

If churches want to play the game of politics, let them pay admission like everyone else.

- George Carlin

I'm completely in favor of the separation of Church and State. My idea is that these two institutions screw us up enough on their own, so both of them together is certain death.

- George Carlin

This magnificent experiment in democracy is just being shredded to pieces by these right-wing Christians. . . . (They're) just shredding the rest of the Bill of Rights which hadn't been shredded already.

- George Carlin

When Evolution is outlawed, only outlaws will evolve.

- George Carlin

I have for many years strictly avoided going to church or having anything to do with Mumbo-Jumbo. We know nothing. All is, and must be, utterly incomprehensible.

- Thomas Carlyle

[Voltaire] gave the death-stab to modern superstition. That horrid incubus, which dwelt in darkness, shunning the light, is passing away. . . . It was a most weighty service.

- Thomas Carlyle

I think that money spent upon foreign missions for China is not only money misspent, but that we do a grievous wrong to the Chinese by trying to force our religion upon them against their wishes.

- Andrew Carnegie

More and more I realize we should think less & less of 'Heaven our Home!' more & more of 'Home our Heaven.'

- Andrew Carnegie

Not only had I got rid of the theology and the supernatural, but I had found the truth of evolution.

- Andrew Carnegie

The whole scheme of Christian Salvation is diabolical as revealed by the creeds. An angry God, imagine such a creator of the universe. Angry at what he knew was coming and was himself responsible for. Then he sets himself about to beget a son, in order that the child should beg him to forgive the Sinner. This however he cannot or will not do. He must punish somebody—so the son offers himself up & our creator punishes the innocent youth, never heard of before—for the guilty and became reconciled to us. . . . I decline to accept Salvation from such a fiend.

- Andrew Carnegie

If you weren't indoctrinated into [religion], it sounds like a far-fetched fairy tale.

- Adam Carolla

I'm an atheist. If you were not born into that culture, it seems like the most outlandish thing in the world. Obviously, you could take any Christian and just have them born into fundamentalist Hasidism, and they would be walking around with the beard and the whole getup. If you weren't indoctrinated into that early on, then it makes no sense.

- Adam Carolla

Christianity fully dominated the whole of the Western world from the 5th to the 15th Century, and yet all those years there was no Scientific Revolution.

- Richard Carrier

If reading the Bible does *not* raise profound problems for you as a modern reader, then check with your doctor and enquire about the symptoms of brain death.

- R. P. Carroll

Consider a hypothetical world in which science had developed to something like its current state of progress, but nobody had yet thought of God. It seems unlikely that an imaginative thinker in this world, upon proposing God as a solution to various cosmological puzzles, would be met with enthusiasm.

- Sean M. Carroll

If a designer was designing us, either they're a terrible designer or they've got a great sense of humor, because we're carrying around all sorts of genes that don't work.

- Sean M. Carroll

I wish to argue that religious belief necessarily entails certain statements about how the universe works, that these statements can be judged as scientific hypotheses, and that as such they should be rejected in favor of alternative ways of understanding the universe.

- Sean M. Carroll

We are looking for a complete, coherent, and simple understanding of reality. Given what we know about the universe, there seems to be no reason to invoke God as part of this description.

- Sean M. Carroll

In my living room I would argue for liberalization of abortion laws, divorce laws, and there are times when I would like to express a view on the air. I would love to have taken on Billy Graham. But I'm on TV five nights a week; I have nothing to gain by it and everything to lose.

- Johnny Carson

Before accepting any belief one ought first to follow reason as a guide, for credulity without enquiry is a sure way to deceive oneself.

- Celsus

I'm a complete atheist. I have no religious views myself and no spiritual views, except very watered down humanistic spiritual views. And consciousness is just a fact of life. It's a natural fact of life.

- David Chalmers

I reject the whole Christian religion [and] a presiding or controlling Deity.

- Daniel Henry Chamberlain

I consider myself an atheist.

- Subrahmanyan Chandrasekhar

In Philadelphia, I inadvertently came upon an edition of Robert Ingersoll's *Essays and Lectures*. This was an exciting discovery; his atheism confirmed my own belief that the horrific cruelty of the Old Testament was degrading to the human spirit.

- Charlie Chaplin

I am no Christian.

- Thomas Chatterton

I hated having to go to church.

- Julia Child

It is impossible to exaggerate the evil work theology has done to the world.

- Lydia Maria Child

I am a child of the Enlightenment. I think irrational belief is a dangerous phenomenon, and I try to consciously avoid irrational belief.

- Noam Chomsky

Epicurus set us free from superstitious terrors and delivered us out of captivity.

- Cicero

Reason is the mistress and queen of all things.

- Cicero

The place of religion in our society is an exalted one, achieved through a long tradition of reliance on the home, the church, and the inviolable citadel of the individual heart and mind. We have come to recognize through bitter experience that it is not within the power of government to invade that citadel, whether its purpose or effect be to aid or oppose , to advance or retard. In the relationship between man and religion, the State is firmly committed to a position of neutrality. Through the application of that rule requires interpretation of a delicate sort, the rule itself is clearly and concisely stated in the words of the First Amendment.

- Tom Campbell Clark

Absolutely no religious rites of any kind, relating to any religious faith, should be associated with my funeral.

- Arthur C. Clarke

I remain an aggressive agnostic.

- Arthur C. Clarke

[Lucretius] hit it on the nail when he said that religion was the by-product of fear—a reaction to a mysterious and often hostile universe. For much of human prehistory, it may have been a necessary evil—but why was it so much more evil than necessary—and why did it survive when it was no longer necessary?

- Arthur C. Clarke

One of the great tragedies of mankind is that morality has been hijacked by religion.

- Arthur C. Clarke

Religion is the most malevolent of all mind viruses. We should get rid of it as quick as we can.

- Arthur C. Clarke

I was asked, 'Do you believe in God?' As it happens I do not know whether God exists. I'm much more of an agnostic.

- Nick Clegg

Not only have the 'followers of Christ' made it their rule to hack to bits all those who do not accept their beliefs, they have also ferociously massacred each other, in the name of their common 'religion of love,' under banners proclaiming their faith in Him who had expressly commanded them to love one another.

- Georges Clemenceau

[For women] the very consciousness of their own nature must evoke feelings of shame.

- St. Clement of Alexandria

We are tired of promises, god is deaf, and his church is our worst enemy.

- Voltairine de Cleyre

I don't believe in heaven and hell. I don't know if I believe in God. All I know is that as an individual, I won't allow this life—the only thing I know to exist—to be wasted.

- George Clooney

Gods are fragile things; they may be killed by a whiff of science or a dose of common sense.

- Chapman Cohen

Human society is born in the shadow of religious fear, and in that stage the suppression of heresy is a sacred social duty. Then comes the rise of a priesthood, and the independent thinker is met with punishment in this world and the threat of eternal damnation hereafter. Even today it is from the religious side that the greatest danger to freedom of thought comes. Religion is the last thing man will civilize.

- Chapman Cohen

Not one man in ten thousand has goodness of heart or strength of mind to be an atheist.

- Samuel Taylor Coleridge

The Use of the Understanding, in endeavoring to find out the Meaning of any Proposition whatsoever, in considering the nature and Evidence for or against it, and in judging of it according to the seeming Force or Weakness of the Evidence.

- Anthony Collins

Let us in the name of the Holy Trinity go on sending all the slaves to Europe that can be sold.

- Christopher Columbus

I admire anyone who's genuinely trying to achieve spiritual enlightenment and live a peaceful life. But religious dogma is a barrier to that. The last thing a dogmatist wants is for anyone to be enlightened, any more than a pharmaceutical company wants anybody cured.

- Pat Condell

I found myself segregated in assembly and shunted into another room while everyone said their morning prayers. I didn't mind. The whole pantomime seemed hollow to me even then. Once you become aware of the gulf between what people profess to believe and how they actually behave, it's hard to take any of it seriously.

- Pat Condell

I set out to write a show in order to say something, rather than just as a vehicle for stand-up. It seems to me that fundamentalist Christians, jihadist Muslims and settlement-building Jews are causing more than their share of trouble in the world. World events are being driven by people with apocalyptic delusions, while here in Britain a paralyzing liberal guilt allows religious bigots to use intimidation and violence to stamp out free speech. If you can't get laughs out of all that, you can't get them out of anything.

- Pat Condell

Religion disapproves of original thought the way Dracula does sunlight.

- Pat Condell

Use their tactics if you feel strongly enough. Make a nuisance of yourself. Make an official complaint. Take it to a tribunal. As an atheist you're part of a minority whose beliefs are constantly ignored and marginalized while religious prejudice is pandered to and encouraged, and you have every right to be offended by that. . . . Remember, one person on their own can't do much, but a million people each doing a little every day can change things very quickly.

- Pat Condell

I don't like religion. I think religion is a con.

- Billy Connolly

The ethical view of the universe involves us at last in so many cruel and absurd contradictions . . . that I have come to suspect that the aim of creation cannot be ethical at all.

- Joseph Conrad

Congress shall make no law respecting an establishment of religion, or prohibiting the free exercise thereof; or abridging the freedom of speech, or of the press; or the right of the people peaceably to assemble, and to petition the Government for a redress of grievances.

- The Constitution of the United States of America, Article I, Bill of Rights

Sunday was a day of just so much external restraint as public opinion absolutely demanded. I learned at last, as I came to be about seventeen, that my father was an entire freethinker, as much as I am now. It shocked me much, because he never taught me anything, allowed me to pick up religion from any one around me, and then scolded me because I embraced beliefs which he knew must condemn him. I think this neglect to be honest with children is a terrible evil. I have lost years of thought, and wandered wide and done such unwise conceited things, and encountered risks for soul and body, all of which might have been obviated by his frank teaching.

- Moncure Daniel Conway

Ignorance and superstition ever bear a close and mathematical relation to each other.

- James Fenimore Cooper

Perhaps there will be babblers who claim to be judges of astronomy although completely ignorant of the subject and, badly distorting some passage of Scripture to their purpose, will dare to find fault with my undertaking and censure it. I disregard them even to the extent of despising their criticism as unfounded.

- Copernicus

To explain the creative musician's basic objective in elementary terms, I would say that a composer writes music to express and communicate and put down in permanent form certain thoughts, emotions and states of being. These thoughts and emotions are gradually formed by the contact of the composer's personality with the world in which he lives. He expresses these thoughts . . . in the musical language of his own time.

- Aaron Copland

I was sent to Sunday school for a few weeks but I didn't like getting up on Sunday mornings.

- Brian Cox

The problem with today's world is that everyone believes they have the right to express their opinion AND have others listen to it. The correct statement of individual rights is that everyone has the right to an opinion, but crucially, that opinion can be roundly ignored and even made fun of, particularly if it is demonstrably nonsense!

- Brian Cox

As the years went on I gradually transmogrified from being an evolutionary biologist to an evolutionary biologist atheist and now I'm more of an atheist than an evolutionary biologist. I realized that creationism, the opposition to evolution, is the least of our worries that religion promulgates, compared to someone throwing acid in the face of a schoolgirl in Afghanistan.

- Jerry Coyne

In physics we don't start off with how we know that atoms exist. In chemistry we don't start off with the evidence for chemical bonds. But evolution is different, because the evidence is so cool and not a lot of people know it, but also because I want you to go out into the world knowing that it's important that this is a fact, it's a true fact about where we came from.

- Jerry Coyne

If some of the Bible is manifestly wrong, why should any of the rest of it be accepted automatically?

- Francis Crick

I realized early on that it is detailed scientific knowledge which makes certain religious beliefs untenable. A knowledge of the true age of the earth and of the fossil record makes it impossible for any balanced intellect to believe in the literal truth of every part of the Bible in the way that fundamentalists do. And if some of the Bible is manifestly wrong, why should any of the rest of it be accepted automatically? . . . What could be more foolish than to base one's entire view of life on ideas that, however plausible at the time, now appear to be quite erroneous? And what would be more important than to find our true place in the universe by removing one by one these unfortunate vestiges of earlier beliefs?

- Francis Crick

I was a skeptic, an agnostic, with a strong inclination toward atheism.

- Francis Crick

When I told the people of Northern Ireland that I was an atheist, a woman in the audience stood up and said, 'Yes, but is it the God of the Catholics or the God of the Protestants in whom you don't believe?'

- Quentin Crisp

[I am] not just an atheist, but a total nonbeliever.

- David Cronenberg

I'm simply a nonbeliever and have been forever. . . . I'm interested in saying, 'Let us discuss the existential question. We are all going to die, that is the end of all consciousness. There is no afterlife. There is no God. Now what do we do.' That's the point where it starts getting interesting to me.

- David Cronenberg

I was born Jewish, but I am an atheist. I don't believe in God.

- David Cross

We can only proceed, individually and collectively, to make whatever improvements are possible in our respective areas of concern, sustained by the hope that others are doing the same.

- Eglin Culhane

The Cambridge ladies who live in furnished souls are unbeautiful and have comfortable minds (also, with the church's protestant blessings daughters, unscented shapeless spirited) they believe in Christ and Longfellow, both dead.

- E. E. Cummings

Pierre belonged to no religion and I did not practice any.

- Marie Curie

# DALY

A woman's asking for equality in the church would be comparable to a black person's demanding equality in the Ku Klux Klan.

- Mary Daly

'God's plan' is often a front for men's plans and a cover for inadequacy, ignorance, and evil.

- Mary Daly

If God is male, then male is God. The divine patriarch castrates women as long as he is allowed to live on in the human imagination

- Mary Daly

We're apes—do apes go anyplace [when they die]?

- Rodney Dangerfield

I'm definitely against all organized religion just because, when you really look at it, organized religion has caused most of the deaths in the history of this planet. Most of the wars were fought over organized religion.

- Sean Danielsen

I do not consider it an insult, but rather a compliment to be called an agnostic. I do not pretend to know where many ignorant men are sure—that is all that agnosticism means.

- Clarence Darrow

I don't believe in God because I don't believe in Mother Goose.

- Clarence Darrow

If today you can take a thing like evolution and make it a crime to teach it in the public school, tomorrow you can make it a crime to teach it in the private schools, and the next year you can make it a crime to teach it to the hustings or in the church. At the next session you may ban books and the newspapers. Soon you may set Catholic against Protestant and Protestant against Protestant, and try to foist your own religion upon the minds of men. If you can do one you can do the other. Ignorance and fanaticism is ever busy and needs feeding. Always it is feeding and gloating for more. Today it is the public school teachers, tomorrow the private. The next day the preachers and the lectures, the magazines, the books, the newspapers. After a while, your honor, it is the setting of man against man and creed against creed until with flying banners and beating drums we are marching backward to the glorious ages of the sixteenth century when bigots lighted fagots to burn the men who dared to bring any intelligence and enlightenment and culture to the human mind.

- Clarence Darrow

Religion is the belief in future life and in God. I don't believe in either.

- Clarence Darrow

I can indeed hardly see how anyone ought to wish Christianity to be true; for if so the plain language of the text seems to show that the men who do not believe, and this would include my Father, Brother, and almost all my best friends, will be everlastingly punished. And this is a damnable doctrine.

- Charles Darwin

The only way I can write—whether that's good or bad—is to put my worldview into everything. I have to challenge that worldview from time to time, but in terms of the atheism of the show, I find that very powerful.

- Russell T. Davies

Yes, I'm deeply atheist.

- Russell T. Davies

As if it were not enough that we fasten belief-labels on babies at birth, those badges of mental apartheid are now reinforced and refreshed. In their separate schools, children are separately taught mutually incompatible beliefs.

- Richard Dawkins

I offered an analogy which teachers might us to bring home to their pupils the true antiquity of the universe. If a history were written at a rate of one century per page, how thick would the book of the universe be? In the view of a Young Earth Creationist, the whole history of the universe, on this scale, would fit comfortably into a slender paperback. And the scientific answer to the question? To accommodate all the volumes of history on the same scale, you'd need a bookshelf ten miles long. That gives the order of magnitude of the yawning gap between true science on the one hand, and the creationist teaching of favored by some schools on the other. This is not some disagreement of scientific detail. It is the difference between single paperback and a library of a million books.

- Richard Dawkins

My respect for the Abrahamic religions went up in the smoke and choking dust of September 11th. The last vestige of respect for the taboo disappeared as I watched the 'Day of Prayer' in Washington Cathedral, where people of mutually incompatible faiths united in homage to the very force that caused the problem in the first place: religion. It is time for people of intellect, as opposed to people of faith, to stand up and say 'Enough!' Let our tribute to the dead be a new resolve: to respect people for what they individually think, rather than respect groups for what they were collectively brought up to believe.

- Richard Dawkins

The god of the Old Testament is arguably the most unpleasant character in all fiction.

- Richard Dawkins

To fill a world with religion, or religions of the Abrahamic kind, is like littering the streets with loaded guns. Do not be surprised if they are used.

- Richard Dawkins

We are all atheists about most of the gods humanity has ever believed in—some of us just go one god further.

- Richard Dawkins

I look forward to receiving 20 emails saying, 'Hey, I noticed you're not religious. Look at your fingerprint. Doesn't that prove that there is a creator, because your fingerprint is completely unique.' Um, no. Doesn't.

- Alex Day

Man enjoys the great advantage of having a God endorse the codes he writes; and since man exercises a sovereign authority over a woman, it is especially fortunate that this authority has been vested in his by the Supreme Being. For the Jews, Mohammedans, and the Christians, among others, man is master by divine right; the fear of God, therefore, will repress any impulse toward revolt in the downtrodden female.

- Simone de Beauvoir

If I were hungry and friendless today, I would rather take my chances with a saloon-keeper than with the average preacher.

- Eugene V. Debs

I left that church with rich and royal hatred of the priest as a person, and a loathing for the church as an institution, and I vowed that I would never go inside a church again.

- Eugene V. Debs

The press and the pulpit have in every age and every nation been on the side of the exploiting class and the ruling class.

- Eugene V. Debs

I do not practice religion in accordance with the sacred rites. I have made mysterious Nature my religion. I do not believe that a man is any nearer to God for being clad in priestly garments, nor that one place in a town is better adapted to meditation than another. When I gaze at a sunset sky and spend hours contemplating its marvelous ever-changing beauty, an extraordinary emotion overwhelms me. Nature in all its vastness is truthfully reflected in my sincere though feeble soul. Around me are the trees stretching up their branches to the skies, the perfumed flowers gladdening the meadow, the gentle grass-carpeted earth, . . . and my hands unconsciously assume an attitude of adoration. . . . To feel the supreme and moving beauty of the spectacle to which Nature invites her ephemeral guests! . . . that is what I call prayer.

- Claude Debussy

The question of souls is old—we demand our bodies, now. We are tired of promises, god is deaf, and his church is our worst enemy.

- Voltairine de Cleyre

It would be an exaggeration to say I'm not afraid of death, but I'm not afraid of what comes after, because I'm not a believer.

- Christian de Duve

Religious faith is experienced emotionally in the depth of personality, while religious beliefs entail the intellectual component of acceptance of dogma. Convictions may have stronger roots than beliefs and may persist in spite of their demonstrated falsehood.

- Jose M. R. Delgado

God? I don't know him. Given a young composer of genius, the surest way to ruin him is to make a Christian of him.

- Frederick Delius

In 1775 there was an earthquake in Lisbon. Thirty thousand people were destroyed in a few minutes! How do you reconcile your loving God who is supposed to mark the fall of every sparrow?

54

- Frederick Delius

Men of simple understanding, little inquisitive and little instructed, make good Christians.

- Michel de Montaigne

The United States is not a religious state, it is a secular state that tolerates all religions and—yes—all manner of nonreligious ethical beliefs as well.

- Daniel Dennett

Politicians don't think they even have to pay us lip service, and leaders who wouldn't be caught dead making religious or ethnic slurs don't hesitate to disparage the 'godless' among us.

- Daniel Dennett

The time has come for us brights to come out of the closet. What is a bright? A bright is a person with a naturalist as opposed to a supernaturalist world view. We brights don't believe in ghosts or elves or the Easter Bunny—or God. We disagree about many things, and hold a variety of views about morality, politics and the meaning of life, but we share a disbelief in black magic—and life after death.

- Daniel Dennett

The court's right wing seems determined to chip away at the wall of separation by limiting the right of citizens to challenge governmental actions that favor Christianity over other religions and over the views of citizens who do not subscribe to any religion.

- Alan Dershowitz

Have not some religions, including the most influential forms of Christianity, taught that the heart of man is totally corrupt? How could the course of religion in its entire sweep not be marked by practices that are shameful in their cruelty and lustfulness, and by beliefs that are degraded and intellectually incredible? What else than what we can find could be expected, in the case of people having little knowledge and no secure method of knowing; with primitive institutions, and with so little control of natural forces that they lived in a constant state of fear?

- John Dewey

I loved God for 25 years, but yet in my search was not able to find any true evidence or proof of his existence or intervention.

- Jerry DeWitt

Pretending has an adult word that we call faith. What religion calls faith is really pretending to believe.

- Jerry DeWitt

Skepticism is my nature, freethought is my methodology, agnosticism is my conclusion after 25 years of being in the ministry, and atheism is my opinion.

- Jerry DeWitt

From fanaticism to barbarism is only one step.

- Denis Diderot

Skepticism is the first step toward truth.

- Denis Diderot

Wandering in a vast forest at night, I have only a faint light to guide me. A stranger appears and says to me: 'My friend, you should blow out your candle in order to find your way more clearly.' This stranger is a theologian.

- Denis Diderot

I lost my faith during the war and can't believe they are all up there, flying around or sitting at tables, all those I've lost.

- Marlene Dietrich

I'm an atheist. . . . how unfortunate it is to assign responsibility to the higher up for justice amongst people.

- Ani DiFranco

I'm not a religious person myself. I'm an atheist. I think religion serves a lot of different purposes in people's lives . . . but then, of course, institutional religions are so problematic.

- Ani DiFranco

Religion is such a medieval idea. Don't get me started. I have thought about every facet of religion and I can't buy any of it.

- Phyllis Diller

Obviously, all religions get corrupted by man. The initial ideas are interesting, but once they get organized, they seem to become about politics and other things and they get misinterpreted. . . . Have faith, but do the work. Live your life right. Don't expect things to happen. That's why I'm put off by magical realism.

- Matt Dillon

Africa, amongst the continents, will teach it to you: that God and the Devil are one, the majestic co-eternal, not two uncreated but one uncreated, and the Natives neither co-founded the persons nor divided the substance.

- Isak Dinesen

If we are honest—and scientists have to be—we must admit that religion is a jumble of false assertions, with no basis in reality. The very idea of God is a product of the human imagination. If religion is still being taught, it is by no means because its ideas still convince us, but simply because some of us want to keep the lower classes quiet.

- Paul Dirac

Even as the church must fear Christ Jesus, so must the wives also fear their husbands. And this inward fear must be shewed by an outward meekness and lowliness in her speeches and carriage to her husband. . . . For if there be not fear and reverence in the inferior, there can be no sound nor constant honor yielded to the superior.

- John Dod

The second duty of the wife is constant obedience and subjection.

- John Dod

I can't embrace a male god who has persecuted female sexuality throughout the ages, and that persecution still goes on today all over the world.

- Amanda Donohoe

I say I'm an atheist but I wouldn't mind being visited by a ghost.

- Natalie Dormer

I prayed for twenty years but received no answer until I prayed with my legs.

- Frederick Douglass

It is a capital mistake to theorize before one has data. Insensibly one begins to twist facts to suit theories, instead of theories to suit facts.

- Arthur Conan Doyle

Women will be saved by going back to that role that God has chosen for them. Ladies, if the hair on the back of your neck stands up it is because you are fighting your role in the scripture.

- Mark Driscoll

Contrary to the fantasies of the fundamentalists, there was no deathbed conversion, no last minute refuge taken in a comforting vision of a heaven or an afterlife. For Carl, what mattered most was what was true, not merely what would make us feel better. Even at this moment when anyone would be forgiven for turning away from the reality of our situation, Carl was unflinching. As we looked deeply into each other's eyes, it was with a shared conviction that our wondrous life together was ending forever.

- Ann Druyan

I don't have any faith, but I have a lot of hope, and I have a lot of dreams of what we could do with our intelligence if we had the will and the leadership and the understanding of how we could take all of our intelligence and our resources and create a world for our kids that is hopeful.

- Ann Druyan

I think that Carl's voice . . . was a great, great service to our culture and to our society, because not only did he convey the importance of skepticism, but also the importance of wonder, too: to have both wonder and skepticism at the same time. People think that if you are a scientist you have to give up that joy of discovery, that passion, that sense of the great romance of life. I say that's completely opposite of the truth. The fact is that the real thing is far more dazzling, far more goose-bump-raising, than any myth or childish story that we can make up.

- Ann Druyan

I flatly refused again to join any church or sign any church creed. From my 30th year on I have increasingly regarded the church as an institution which defended such evils as slavery, color caste, exploitation of labor and war.

- W. E. B. Du Bois

And [Buddhism] deals with the fact, in essence, you know, come right out and say it, that there is no God, that the individual is God.

- Patrick Duffy

I don't believe lies!

- Isadora Duncan

Secular multi-culturalists are not the enemies of religion. We are its defenders. Unless each religion is kept in check, it threatens the others.

- Ian Dunt

Does history support a belief in God? If by God we mean not the creative vitality of nature but a supreme being intelligent and benevolent, the answer must be a reluctant negative.

- Ariel Durant

We never deserted our faith for any other, but we lost most of it as we rubbed against a harsh and increasingly secular world. . . . My Uncle Maurice helped to free me from such nonsense, and awoke in me a desire to read books and enter the world of thought.

- Ariel Durant

By the end of my sophomore year, I had discovered, through Darwin and other infidels, that the difference between man and the gorilla is largely a matter of trousers and words; that Christianity was only one of a hundred religions claiming special access to truth and salvation; and that myths of virgin births, mother goddesses, dying and resurrected deities, had appeared in many pre-Christian faiths, and had helped to transform a lovable Hebrew mystic into the Son of God.

- Will Durant

Religious force is nothing other than the collective and anonymous force of the clan.

- Emile Durkheim

Archeology digs the Bible's grave.

- Steve Dustcircle

Cop-out excuses and catch-phrase dismissals can only work so long before the holes in the religious argument cannot be ignored any longer.

- Steve Dustcircle

# ECCLESTON

I'm an atheist. . . . There was no defining moment in which I decided there was no god for me. It was more of a growing process. I do feel that whatever religious beliefs I had as a child were foisted upon me. It's like when you ask me where Grandma went when she died, and you'd be told that she went to heaven. I wouldn't necessarily view that as a bad thing, but it was stuff like that which I think hindered my intellectual development. Now that I've grown, I prefer a different interpretation.

- Christopher Eccleston

I cannot believe in the immortality of the soul. . . . I am an aggregate of cells, as, for instance, New York City is an aggregate of individuals. Will New York City go to heaven? . . . No; nature made us—nature did it all—not the gods of the religions.

- Thomas Alva Edison

If there is no God, does that mean that life has no purpose? Does it mean that personal existence ends at death? They are thoughts that do my head in. One thing that I can say, however, is that even if I am unable to discover some fundamental purpose to life, this will not give me a reason to return to Christianity. Just because something is unpalatable does not mean that it is not true.

- Jonathan Edwards

I was always dismissive of sports psychology when I was competing, but I now realize that my belief in God was sports psychology in all but name.

- Jonathan Edwards

Much of human progress has been in defiance of religion or of the apparent natural order. The defiance of religious and secular authority has led to democracy, human rights, and the protection of the environment. Humanists make no apologies for this.

Humanists twist no biblical doctrine to justify such actions.

- Fred Edwords

I believe in Spinoza's God, who reveals himself in the orderly harmony in being, not in God who deals with the facts and actions of men.

- Albert Einstein

I cannot imagine a God who rewards and punishes the objects of his creation, whose purposes are modeled after our own—a God, in short, who is but a reflection of human frailty. Neither can I believe that the individual survives the death of his body, although feeble souls harbor such thoughts through fear or ridiculous egotism. It is enough for me to contemplate the mystery of conscious life perpetuating itself through all eternity, to reflect upon the marvelous structure of the universe which we can dimly perceive, and to try humbly to comprehend even an infinitesimal part of the intelligence manifested in nature.

- Albert Einstein

I do not believe in a personal God and I have never denied this but have expressed it clearly. If something is in me which can be called religious then it is the unbounded admiration for the structure of the world so far as our science can reveal it.

- Albert Einstein

In their struggle for the ethical good, teachers of religion must have the stature to give up the doctrine of a personal God, that is, give up that source of fear and hope which in the past placed such vast power in the hands of priests. In their labors they will have to avail themselves of those forces which are capable of cultivating the Good, the True, and the Beautiful in humanity itself. This is, to be sure a more difficult but an incomparably more worthy task.

- Albert Einstein

This insight into the mystery of life, coupled though it be with fear, also has given rise to religion. To know that what is impenetrable to us really exists, manifesting itself as the highest wisdom and the most radiant beauty which our dull faculties can comprehend only in their primitive forms—this knowledge, this feeling, is at the center of true religiousness. In this sense, and in this sense only, I belong in the ranks of devoutly religious men.

- Albert Einstein

The clergy are, practically, the most irresponsible of all talkers.

- George Eliot

Christians, like other religionists, are not so much convinced by their arguments and proofs as colonized by assumptions and premises. As a form of culture, it seems self-evident to them; they are not so much indoctrinated as enculturated.

- David Eller

For a man to be a true believer and to be strong and independent is impossible; religion and self-sufficiency are contradictory terms.

- Albert Ellis

[Religion's] absolutistic, perfectionistic thinking is the prime creator of the two most corroding of human emotions: anxiety and hostility.

- Albert Ellis

We can have no certainty that God does or does not exist [but] we have an exceptionally high degree of probability that he or she doesn't.

- Albert Ellis

Had there been a Lunatic Asylum in the suburbs of Jerusalem, Jesus Christ would infallibly have been shut up in it at the outset of his public career. That interview with Satan on a pinnacle of the Temple would alone have damned him, and everything that happened after could have confirmed the diagnosis. The whole religious complexion of the modern world is due to the absence from Jerusalem of a Lunatic Asylum.

- Henry Havelock Ellis

I find nothing more ridiculous and annoying than some guy who runs a kickoff back 105 yards from the end zone and drops to his knees and thanks God. Well, that's foolish. God didn't do it. He did it. Because if God did that for him, you mean God was against the other team? God is that mean-spirited that he has nothing better to do on Sunday afternoon than beat the crap out of a bunch of poor football players? I don't believe in the universe being run by that kind of a God. I go with Mark Twain.

- Harlan Ellison

I think [religion] is presumptuous and I think it is silly, because it makes you believe that you are less than what you can be. As long as you can blame everything on some unseen deity, you don't ever have to be responsible for your own behavior.

- Harlan Ellison

The dull pray; the geniuses are light mockers.

- Ralph Waldo Emerson

What I want to indicate by the word godless is not only god in the religious sense but I am trying to accept and enjoy the idea that we never will reach that condition of agreement of certainty, that actually we're unanchored, we're floating around, and we're actually guessing. That's what we're doing. Everyone is making guesses, and trying to make the best of it, watching what happens and being empirical about it. There won't be a plan, so godless, like most of those words, have a lot of resonance for me. They are words I find myself using in conversation sometimes, over and over again.

- Brian Eno

Is God willing to prevent evil, but not able? Then he is not omnipotent. Is he able, but not willing? then he is malevolent. Is he both able and willing? Then whence cometh evil? Is he neither able nor willing? Then why call him God?

- Epicurus

The gods can either take away evil from the world and will not, or, being willing to do so cannot; or they neither can nor will, or lastly, they are able and willing. If they have the will to remove evil and cannot, then they are not omnipotent. If they can but will not, then they are not benevolent. If they are neither able nor willing, they are neither omnipotent nor benevolent. Lastly, if they are both able and willing to annihilate evil, why does it exist?

- Epicurus

My dad, who was a devout atheist, had once told my mom that he wanted his remains to be thrown out in the trash.

- Hugh Everett III

# FAHRINGER

I said to my husband, 'I can't teach this stuff to my kids. I'm nicer than God.

- Catherine Fahringer

We would be 1,500 years ahead if it hadn't been for the church dragging science back by its coattails and burning our best minds at the stake.

- Catherine Fahringer

I wondered why God was such a useless thing. It seemed a waste of of time to have him. After that he became less and less, until he was . . . nothingness.

- Frances Farmer

I felt rather proud to think that I had found the truth myself, without help from anyone. It puzzled me that other people hadn't found out, too.

- Frances Farmer

The sooner you get rid of all this Christian humbug the better. The whole traditional concept of life is false. Throw the great Christian blinkers away, and look around you and stand on your own feet. . . . Don't believe all the tommyrot priests tell you; learn and prove everything by your own experience. . . . One thing is for certain—that English music will never be any good till they get rid of Jesus. Humanity is incredible. It will believe anything, anything to escape reality.

- Eric Fenby

I am better known for my unbelief than any man in the territory, except [fellow Montana pioneer] Granville Stuart.

- James Fergus

I have come to the conclusion that there is not enough money in

Scotland to make me tell a lie.

- James Fergus

Religion is declining, with no better proof than I am here today. Two hundred years ago, I would have been burned at the stake. What was considered hearsay by our fathers is tolerated now. The hell that frightened us in childhood has vanished into space. Heaven is not in our geographies. Therefore, we see the old faiths loosing their hold on the human mind.

- James Fergus

The Christian religion brought about a long period of ignorance still known to us as the dark ages, during which thought was curbed, common education banished, and conscience given over to a rude, vulgar and ignorant priesthood. And whatever good Christianity may have done since, much of the degeneracy of mankind during this period must be laid at its door.

- James Fergus

I'm still a nonbeliever, even though my idea of reason is the idea of a reason which is open to mystery.

- Giuliano Ferrara

I thought nature itself was so interesting that I didn't want it distorted (by miracle stories). And so I gradually came to disbelieve the whole religion.

- Richard Feynman

Start out understanding religion by saying everything is possibly wrong. . . . As son as you do that, you start sliding down an edge which is hard to recover from.

- Richard Feynman

Prayers never bring anything. . . . They may bring solace to the sap, the bigot, the ignorant, and the lazy—but to the enlightened it is the same as asking Santa Claus to bring you something for Xmas.

- W. C. Fields

Forget believing in God. How about thinking for yourself on any subject! Bottom line—I don't care what you believe, or what church you attend, or how religion-oriented your private life is. Keep it out of my government. Keep it out of my laws. Keep it out of my bedroom. And keep it out of the war rooms at the Pentagon!

- Harvey Fierstein

I don't believe in heaven. In fact, I don't believe in any sort of conscious afterlife. More to the point, I don't believe in God. Or Gods. Or Goddesses. . . . More wars have been fought in the name of religion than any other cause. More people have been persecuted, reputations ruined, and fortunes plundered and murders committed in the name of religion than any other enterprise. And more everyday bigotry and prejudice is founded on what religion a person follows than any other factor.

- Harvey Fierstein

No, but I am Jewish. . . . This [performance] has really brought out the Jew. I mean, I don't believe in God, I don't believe in heaven or hell, but I pray three or four times a day.

- Harvey Fierstein

We are lucky enough to be living in a country that not only guarantees the freedom to practice religion as we see fit, but also freedom *from* religious zealots who would persecute and prosecute and even physically harm those of us who do not believe as they do. . . . If you refuse to salute the flag and say God in your pledge, you're actually judged un-American. But that's not the way America is supposed to be. That's the way Iran is. . . . Predicating patriotism on a citizen's belief in God is as anti-American as judging him on the color of his skin. It is wrong. It is useless. It is unconstitutional.

- Harvey Fierstein

But be sweet to your mother at Xmas despite her early Chaldean rune-worship which she will undoubtedly inflict on you at Xmas.

- F. Scott Fitzgerald

I can't admit of an old boy God who takes walks in his garden with a cane in his hand, who lodges his friends in the belly of whales, dies uttering a cry, and rises again after three days; things absurd in themselves, and completely opposed, moreover, to all physical laws, which proves to us, by the way, that priests have always wallowed in squalid ignorance, and tried to drag whole nations down after them.

- Gustave Flaubert

With an absolute God, his word revealed and his will eternal, how could relativity in ethics get anywhere with them?

- Joseph Fletcher

There had never been any renunciation of religion on my part, but life so many people, it was a gradual fading away.

- Henry Fonda

The merits and services of Christianity have been industriously extolled by its hired advocates. Every Sunday its praises are sounded from myriads of pulpits. It enjoys the prestige of an ancient establishment and the comprehensive support of the State. It has the ear of rulers and the control of education. Every generation is suborned in its favor. Those who dissent from it are losers, those who oppose it are ostracized; while in the past, for century after century, it has replied to criticism with imprisonment, and to skepticism with the dungeon and the stake. By such means it has induced a general tendency to allow its pretensions without inquiry and its beneficence without proof.

- G. W. Foote (and J. M. Wheeler)

Who burnt heretics? Who roasted or drowned millions of 'witches'? Who built dungeons and filled them? Who brought forth cries of agony from honest men and women that rang the tingling stars? Who burnt Bruno? Who spat filth over the graves of Paine and Voltaire? The answer is one word—*Christians*.

- G. W. Foote

Government in our democracy, state and national, must be neutral in matters of religious theory, doctrine, and practice.

- Abe Fortas

I absolutely believe what Ellie [Arroway, the atheist astronomer in the movie "Contact"] believes—that there is no direct evidence, so how could you ask me to believe in God when there's absolutely no evidence that I can see? I do believe in the beauty and the awe-inspiring mystery of the science that's out there that we haven't discovered yet, that there are scientific explanations for phenomena that we call mystical because we don't know any better.

- Jodie Foster

Shameful rivalries of creed

Shall not make the martyr bleed

In the good time coming

Religion shall be shorn of pride

And flourish all the stronger;

And Charity shall trim her lamp;

Wait a little longer.

- Stephen Foster

The Holiness of God is not evidenced in women when they are brash, brassy, boisterous, brazen, head-strong, strong-willed, loud-mouthed, overly-talkative, having to have the last word, challenging, controlling, manipulative, critical, conceited, arrogant, aggressive, assertive, strident, interruptive, undisciplined, insubordinate, disruptive, dominating, domineering, or clamoring for power. Rather, women accept

70

God's holy order and character by being humbly and unobtrusively respectful and receptive in functional subordination to God, church leadership, and husbands.

- James Fowler

Being an atheist is a matter not of moral choice, but of human obligation.

- John Fowles

The impotence of God is infinite.

- Anatole France

The thoughts of the gods are not more unchangeable than those of the men who interpret them. They advance—but they always lag behind the thoughts of men. . . . The Christian God was once a Jew. Now he an anti-Semite.

- Anatole France

Separation means separation, not something less. Jefferson's metaphor in describing the relation between Church and State speaks of a 'wall of separation,' not a fine line easily overstepped. The public school is at once the symbol of our democracy and the most pervasive means for promoting our common destiny. In no activity of the State is it more vital to keep out divisive forces than in its schools, to avoid confusing, not to say fusing, what the Constitution sought to keep strictly apart. 'The great American principle of eternal separation'—Elihu Root's phrase bears repetition—is one of the vital reliances of our Constitutional system for assuring unities among our people stronger than our diversities. It is the Court's duty to enforce this principle in its full integrity.

- Justice Frankfurter

If we look back into history for the character of the present sects in Christianity, we shall find few that have not in their turns been persecutors, and complainers of persecution. The primitive Christians thought persecution extremely wrong in the Pagans, but practiced it on one another. The first Protestants of the Church of England blamed persecution in the Romish Church, but practiced it upon the Puritans. They found it wrong in Bishops, but fell into the practice themselves both here (England) and in New England.

- Benjamin Franklin

Lighthouses are more helpful then churches.

- Benjamin Franklin

The way to see by faith is to shut the eye of reason.

- Benjamin Franklin

When a religion is good, I conceive it will support itself; and when it does not support itself, and God does not care to support it so that its professors are obliged to call for help of the civil power, 'tis a sign, I apprehend, of its being a bad one.

- Benjamin Franklin

Religion is the idol of the mob; it adores everything it does not understand. . . . We know the crimes that fanaticism in religion caused.

- Frederick the Great

A religion, even if it calls itself the religion of love, must be hard and unloving to those who do not belong to it.

- Sigmund Freud

Religion is comparable to a childhood neurosis.

- Sigmund Freud

[Religion's] doctrines carry with them the stamp of the times in which they originated, the ignorant childhood days of the human race. Its consolations deserve no trust.

- Sigmund Freud

You cannot exaggerate the intensity of man's inner resolution and craving for authority.

- Sigmund Freud

Guilt feelings have proved to be the most effective means of forming and increasing dependency, and herein lies one of the social functions of authoritarian ethics throughout society.

- Erich Fromm

In faith cannot be reconciled with rational thinking, it has to be eliminated as an anachronistic remnant of earlier stages of culture and replaced by science dealing with facts and theories which are intelligible and can be validated.

- Erich Fromm

In observing the quality of thinking in alienated man, it is striking to see how his intelligence has developed and how reason has deteriorated. . . . Even from the nineteenth century to our day, there seems to have occurred an observable increase in stupidity, if by this we mean the opposite to reason, rather than to intelligence.

- Erich Fromm

To the degree to which a person conforms he cannot hear the voice of his conscience, much less act upon it.

- Erich Fromm

I turned to speak to God about the world's despair, but to make matters worse I found God wasn't there.

- Robert Frost

The kind of Unitarian—who having by elimination got from many gods to three, and three to one—thinks why not taper off to none at all.

- Robert Frost

I love how when people watch I don't know, David Attenborough or Discovery Planet type thing you know where you see the absolute phenomenal majesty and complexity and bewildering beauty of nature and you stare at it and then . . . somebody next to you goes, 'And how can you say there is no God? Look at that.' And then five minutes later you're looking at the life-cycle of a parasitic worm whose job is to bury itself in the eyeball of a little lamb and eat the eyeball from inside while the lamb dies in horrible agony and then you turn to them and say, 'Yeah, where is your God now?'

- Stephen Fry

Religion is one of the important questions in life, I think. Or the disposition of our mortal souls and what happens to us after we die, and whether there is or isn't a God. I definitely think about it every day of my life. Given that it's that important a topic, it just makes sense to deal with it in music. . . . I'm not really a confirmed atheist. But I am kind of a reluctant disbeliever.

- Robbie Fulks

Give me truth; cheat me by no illusion.

- Margaret Fuller

# GAGE

During the ages, no rebellion has been of like importance with that of Woman against the tyranny of the Church and State; none has had its far reaching effects.

- Matilda Joslyn Gage

In order to help preserve the very life of the Republic, it is imperative that women should unite upon a platform of opposition to the teaching and aim of that ever most unscrupulous enemy of freedom—the Church.

- Matilda Joslyn Gage

There is a word sweeter than Mother, Home, or Heaven; that word is Liberty.

- Matilda Joslyn Gage

I have managed most of my life to exclude religious speculation from my mode of thought. I've found that, on the whole, it adds very little to economics.

- John Kenneth Galbraith

I have been . . . suspected of heresy, that is, of having held and believed that the Sun is the center of the universe and immovable, and that the earth is not the center of the same, and that it does move. . . . I abjure with a sincere heart and unfeigned faith, I curse and detest the said errors and heresies, and generally all and every error and sect contrary to the Holy Catholic church.

- Galileo Galilei

Clericalism, that's the enemy!

- Leon Gambetta

There exists no politician in India daring enough to attempt to explain to the masses that cows can be eaten.

- Indira Gandhi

Don't bow before another person or another nation.

- Mahatma Gandhi

What difference does it make to the dead, the orphans, and the homeless, whether the mad destruction is wrought under the name of totalitarianism or the holy name of liberty and democracy.

- Mahatma Gandhi

[Gerald] was an activist atheist, a proselytizing atheist. He thought that not saying you were an atheist hurt the cause of reality.

- Jo Ann Evans-Gardner

Bad science contributes to the steady dumbing down of our nation. Crude beliefs get transmitted to political leaders and the result is considerable damage to society. We see this happening now in the rapid rise of the religious right and how it has taken over large segments of the Republican Party. I think fundamentalist and Pentecostalist Pat Robertson is a far greater menace to America than, say, Jesse Helms who will soon be gone and forgotten.

- Martin Gardner

I grew up believing that the Bible was a revelation straight from God. . . . It lasted about halfway through my years at the University of Chicago.

- Martin Gardner

Dear Friends, Man has created God; not God man.

- Giuseppe Garibaldi

[God] just seems very man-made to me. There are so many theories, and not everyone can be right. It's human nature to need a religious crutch, and I don't begrudge anyone that. I just don't need one.

- Janeane Garofalo

Organized religions and their dogmas only serve to indoctrinate the participants into sheep-like common behaviors. This type of blind assimilation promotes the popularity of top-forty count down radio stations and movie sequels. Skepticism towards groups, holy or otherwise, is enriching and makes you a far more entertaining person.

- Janeane Garofalo

The most determined opposition it encounters is from the clergy generally, whose teachings of the Bible are intensely inimical to the equality of woman with man.

- Lloyd Garrison

Why go to the Bible [about woman suffrage]? What question was ever settled by the Bible? What question of theology or any other department? The human mind is greater than any book. The mind sits in judgment on every book. If there be truth in the book, we take it; if error, we discard it. Why refer this to the Bible? In this country, the Bible has been used to support slavery and capital punishment; while in the old countries, it has been quoted to sustain all manner of tyranny and persecution. All reforms are anti-Bible.

- Lloyd Garrison

There are no gods, no devils, no angels, no heaven or hell. There is only our natural world. Religion is but myth and superstition that hardens hearts and enslaves minds.

- Anne Nichol Gaylor

There were many groups working for women's rights, but none of them dealt with the root cause of women's oppression—religion.

- Anne Nichol Gaylor

The only true shield standing between women and the bible, that handbook for the subjugation of women, is a secular government.

U.S. citizens must wake up to the threat of an encroaching theocracy, and shore up Thomas Jefferson's 'wall of separation between church and state.'

- Annie Laurie Gaylor

Being an atheist I can't be either [a saint or a sinner].

- Bob Geldof

I actively disliked the Church and its institutionalized morality which I felt bedeviled Ireland.

- Bob Geldof

I was a quarter Catholic, a quarter Protestant, a quarter Jewish and a quarter nothing–the nothing won.

- Bob Geldof

I must note that although I was brought up as a Protestant, I have been an atheist my entire adult life. I do not proselytize, however. Nor do I question the faith of others. I just don't want to be obliged to accept someone else's faith as a factor in my government.

- Jack Germond

No religious doctrine shall be established by law.

- Elbridge Gerry

De t'ings dat yo' li'ble

To read in de Bible

It ain't necessarily so.

- Ira Gershwin

It's always better to tell the truth. The truth doesn't hurt, and saying that, my mother only ever lied to me about one thing. She said there was a God. But that's because when you're a working-class mum, Jesus is like an unpaid babysitter. She thought if I was God-fearing, then I'd be good.

- Ricky Gervais

A state of skepticism and suspense may amuse a few inquisitive minds. But the practice of superstition is so congenial to the multitude that, if they are forcibly awakened, they still regret the loss of their pleasing vision. Their love of the marvelous and supernatural, their curiosity with regard to future events, and their strong propensity to extend their hopes and fears beyond the limits of the visible world, were the principle causes which favored the establishment of Polytheism. So urgent on the vulgar is the necessity of believing, that the fall of any system of mythology will most probably be succeeded by the introduction of some other mode of superstition.

- Edward Gibbon

It was not in this world that the primitive Christians were desirous of making themselves either agreeable or useful.

- Edward Gibbon

These rigid sentiments, which had been unknown to the ancient world, appear to have infused a spirit of bitterness into a system of love and harmony. The ties of blood and friendship were frequently torn asunder by the difference of religious faith; and the Christians, who, in this world, found themselves oppressed by the power of the Pagans, were sometimes seduced by resentment and spiritual pride to delight in the prospect of their future triumph.

- Edward Gibbon

The various forms of worship, which prevailed in the Roman world, were all considered by the people to be equally true, by the philosopher as equally false, and by the magistrate as equally useful.

- Edward Gibbon

The abominable laws respecting [women in the Bible] . . . are a disgrace to civilization and English literature; and my family which permits such a volume to lie on their parlor-table ought to be ostracized from all respectable society.

- Ella E. Gibson

I grew up in the Christian church, a Christian background. I won prizes for catechism, for being able to remember Bible verses. I am steeped in that tradition, but I've made decisions in my adult life about my own views.

- Julia Gillard

I'm not a religious person. I'm of course a great respecter of religious beliefs but they're not my beliefs.

- Julia Gillard

I'm not going to pretend a faith I don't feel.

- Julia Gillard

I've never thought it was the right thing for me to go through religious rituals for the sake of appearance. . . . For people of faith, I think the greatest compliment I could pay them is to respect their genuinely-held beliefs and not to engage in some pretense about mine.

- Julia Gillard

One religion after another has accepted and perpetuated man's original mistake in making a private servant of the mother of the race.

- Charlotte Perkins Gilman

What glory there was in an omnipotent being torturing forever a puny little creature who could in no way defend himself? Would it be to the glory of a man to fry ants?

- Charlotte Perkins Gilman

This earthly heaven is enough for me.

- David Gilmour

When you get to 60, one of your preoccupations is that the life you have ahead of you is quite a lot shorter than the life you have behind you. You can't help thinking about that. It's something inside all of us, even though I'm not a believer in God or an afterlife. I'm an atheist. I'm sort of resigned to my lot in life, and content in it.

- David Gilmour

Although we weren't brought up to be any particular religion, we were taught to say our prayers. I remember one that ended, 'Thy glorious kingdom, which is for ever and ever. Amen.' These words made me scream, 'I don't want to be anywhere for ever and ever. It's too much.'

- Hermione Gingold

I am an atheist, that is, I think nothing exists except and beyond nature. Within the limits of my, undoubtedly insufficient knowledge of the history of philosophy, I do not see in fact any difference between atheism and the pantheism of Spinoza. That is why I think that Einstein was also an atheist, because in 1929, when asked what he believed in, he answered: 'I believe in Spinoza's God, who shows himself in the harmony of all that exists, but not in a God who takes care of the fate and actions of people.' Unfortunately, in the post-Soviet time in Russia a clerical offensive has been going on, while the voice of atheists is completely stifled. That is why since 1998 I have been defending atheism in the press, and after being awarded the Nobel Prize I managed to say about that on television as well.

- Vitaly Ginzburg

I enjoin and require that no ecclesiastic, missionary, or minister of any sect whatever shall ever hold or exercise any station or duty whatever in the said college; nor shall any such person ever be admitted for any purpose, or as a visitor, within the premises appropriated to the purpose of the said college. . . . My desire is that all the instructors and teachers in the college shall take pains to instill into the minds of the scholars the purest principles of morality, so that, on their entrance into active life, they may, from inclination and habit, evince benevolence toward their fellow creatures, and a love of truth, sobriety, and industry, adopting at the same time such religious tenets as their matured reason may enable them to prefer.

- Stephen Girard

I found I just didn't believe in God.

- Ira Glass

When you have one picture of the world which includes God and one that doesn't, the one where there is no God just emotionally felt more right to me. It is like knowing that you are in love with this person not that person, and reason or arguing about it won't change that.

- Ira Glass

If you repeat a lie often enough, it becomes the truth.

- Joseph Goebbels

Deceiving oneself is bad enough, but where religious faith becomes really dangerous is when people use it to harm others.

- Benjamin J. Gohs

Hate the theonomy, not the theologist.

- Benjamin J. Gohs

I'm a total atheist, and for me it's just about trying to find something that rises above the banal day-to-day bullshit of living.

- Myla Goldberg

'Blessed are the meek, for they shall inherit the earth.' What a preposterous notion! What incentive to slavery, inactivity, and parasitism!

- Emma Goldman

I do not believe in God, because I believe in man. Whatever his mistakes, man has for thousands of years been working to undo the botched job your god has made. There are, however, some potentates I would kill by any and all means at my disposal. They are Ignorance, Superstition, and Bigotry—the most sinister and tyrannical rulers on earth.

- Emma Goldman

There is no position on which people are so immovable as their religious beliefs. There is no more powerful ally one can claim in a debate than Jesus Christ, or God, or Allah, or whatever one calls this supreme being. The religious factions that are growing throughout our land are not using their religious clout with wisdom. They are trying to force government leaders into following their position 100 percent. If you disagree with these religious groups on a particular moral issue, they complain, they threaten you with a loss of money or votes or both. I'm frankly sick and tired of the political preachers across this country telling me . . . that if I want to be a moral person, I must believe in A, B, C, and D. Just who do they think they are?

- Barry Goldwater

A profession that we are a nation 'under God' is identical to a profession that we are a nation 'under Jesus,' a nation 'under Vishnu,' a nation 'under Zeus,' or a nation 'under no god.'

- Alfred Goodwin

The greatest contribution of atheism is the provision of a firm basis for ethical conduct. Atheism explains that morality is a social obligation but not a passport to heaven and salvation. The theistic belief in divine retribution sidetracked moral behavior. Believers were more prone to please the god of their imagination by prayer and ritual than to conform to rules of moral conduct. Consequently immorality and anti-social activities spread wild wherever people were absorbed in the worship of god and in the propitiation of fate. Atheism brings about radical changes in the outlook of people in this context. Truth, tolerance, love and equality are the basic needs of social harmony.

- Gora (Goparaju Ramachandra Rao)

This 'search for God' business must be forbidden for a time—it is a perfectly useless occupation.

- Maxim Gorky

We are here because one odd group of fishes had a peculiar fin anatomy that could transform into legs for terrestrial creatures; because the earth never froze entirely during an ice age; because a small and tenuous species, arising in Africa a quarter of a million years ago, has managed, so far, to survive by hook and by crook. We may yearn for a 'higher answer'—but none exists.

- Stephen Jay Gould

If you can believe in God, then you can believe in anything. It's a gang mentality.

- Greg Graffin

There is only this life, so live wonderfully and meaningfully.

- Greg Graffin

Leave the matter of religion to the family altar, the Church, and the private schools, supported entirely by private contributions. Keep the church and state forever separate.

- Ulysses S. Grant

There was a time when religion ruled the world. It is known as the Dark Ages.

- Ruth Hurmence Green

[It is] strange beyond anything I can think to be able to believe in any of the known religions.

- Kate Greenaway

I disbelieved in God. If I were ever to be convinced in even the remote possibility of a supreme, omnipotent and omniscient power I realized that nothing afterwards could seem impossible. It was on the ground of dogmatic atheism that I fought and fought hard.

- Graham Greene

I prefer to be an agnostic and think that the body itself produces its own miracle.

- Graham Greene

I've always found it difficult to believe in God. I suppose I'd now call myself a Catholic atheist.

- Graham Greene

When I became a Catholic and had to take another name, I took Thomas, after the doubter.

- Graham Greene

A lot of people come up here and thank Jesus for this award. I want you to know that no one had less to do with this award than Jesus. He didn't help me a bit . . . So all I can say is suck it, Jesus. This award is my god now.

- Kathy Griffin

I can criticize your religion all I want, and you can criticize mine. I don't like this whole climate of, 'You can't ever say anything bad about the group I'm in, cause every group is untouchable.' We can all criticize each other and engage in debate all we want.

- Kathy Griffin

Technically, I'm an agnostic, but I definitely believe in hell—especially after watching the fall TV schedule.

- Matt Groening

I am not Christ or a philanthropist. . . . I am all the contrary of a Christ. . . . I fight for the things I believe in, with the weapons at my disposal and try to leave the other man dead so that I don't get nailed to a cross or any other place.

- Che Guevara

# HAILEY

I'd been on patrol, and I went to church that evening. It was an Anglican church, quite high church (A always liked the ceremony) and I was standing up, reciting the Apostles' Creed (which to this day I could recite word for word) and suddenly I realized I didn't believe a word of it, and probably never had. And I never went back to church after that, except for the occasional funeral.

- Arthur Hailey

I've never met a healthy person who worried much about his health, or a good person who worried much about his soul.

- John B. S. Haldane

Oh, I have plenty of biases, all right. I'm quite biased toward depending upon what my senses and my intellect tell me about the world around me, and I'm quite biased against invoking mysterious mythical beings that other people want to claim exist but which they can offer no evidence for. By telling students that the beliefs of a superstitious tribe thousands of years ago should be treated on an equal basis with the evidence collected with our most advanced equipment today is to completely undermine the entire process of scientific inquiry. And one more thing: In your original message you identified yourself as an elementary school teacher. If you are going to insist on holding to a creationist viewpoint, then please stay away from my children. I want my kids to learn about 'real' science, and how the 'real' world operates, and not be fed the mythical goings-on in the fantasy-land of creationism.

- Alan Hale

Suppose a modern Eve would come

And tempt you with an apple

Say just about the size of these?

Would you temptation grapple

And manfully declare: 'I won't?'

Or, would you say:

'Well, I Think since you've picked them;

They'd be best in dumplings or in a pie.

And, let us ask the serpent in

To share with us at dinner.

A de'il with taste for fruit like that

Can't be a hopeless sinner.

- Sharon Hall

The Christian mentality . . . that one isn't supposed to learn from animals. One is more or less supposed to look down on them, manage them, use them, but not learn from them.

- Frances Hamerstrom

When I was eight years old, I tried prayer. And it didn't work!

- Frances Hamerstrom

You'll notice that our 'pair bond' has lasted fairly well and I think it's because we're both remarkably tolerant people. He's an agnostic and I'm an atheist, and we've put up with each other all this time!

- Frances Hamerstrom

The [*Series of Unfortunate Events*] books have drawn the ire and praise of fundamentalist Christians, some of whom believe the books to be Christian allegories and some of whom believe them to be long insults against Christianity. The thing is, the books are really neither.

- Daniel Handler (Lemony Snicket)

I was getting into theology and studying the roots of the Bible, but then I started to discover the man-made nature of it. I started seeing things that made me ask, 'Is God really speaking through this instrument? . . . My eyes opened to the reality of the Bible being just a document to control people. At the time I was a real mama's boy and deeply mesmerized by the church.

- Woody Harrelson

Some of the best known Bible stories center on King David, yet neither history nor archeology can substantiate any of them.

- Roberta Harris

The bible was written at a time when people thought the Earth was flat, when the wheelbarrow was high tech. Are its teachings applicable to the challenges we now face as a civilization?

- Sam Harris

The scientific community is predominantly secular and liberal—and the concessions that scientists have made to religious dogmatism have been breathtaking.

- Sam Harris

Science and religion—being antithetical ways of thinking about the same reality—will never come to terms.

- Sam Harris

We atheists lead happy lives, never concerned with the-dying-and-burn forever-in-hell nonsense. We know better. We enjoy happiness with our friends and neighbors and ignore all the greed and rituals that pay the parasite priests. Let them wallow in their medieval superstition while we enjoy all the wonders of our God-free universe.

- Harry Harrison

I doubt whether I will ever be anything but an honest Agnostic, because I prefer, as I once told you, to go to the grave with my eyes open.

- Hubert Harrison

It should seem that Negroes, of all Americans, would be found in the Free-thought fold, since they have suffered ore than any other class of Americans from the dubious blessings of Christianity.

- Hubert Harrison

Many people who reject supernatural Christianity nonetheless embrace Christ's message of compassion. [Leo] Tolstoy carried this pattern to an extreme. He renounced organized religion and was excommunicated by the Russian Orthodox Church—yet he became almost a monk, living in service to others.

- James A. Haught

All that my work has shown is that you don't have to say that the way the universe began was the personal whim of God.

- Stephen Hawking

There is a fundamental difference between religion, which is based on authority, [and] science, which is based on observation and reason. Science will win because it works.

- Stephen Hawking

[Herman Melville] can neither believe, nor be comfortable in his unbelief; and he is too honest and courageous not to try to do one or the other. If he were a religious man, he would be truly one of the most truly religious and reverential; he has a very high and noble nature, and better worth immortality than most of us.

- Nathaniel Hawthorne

Your happy atheist advice-maker proudly presents the serenity prayer.

- Carolyn Hax

To me [Christianity] was all nonsense, based on that profane compilation of fables called the Bible.

- Bill Haywood

Almost all the great poets have conversations in their poetry about doubting God, and even go all the way to dismissing. It's such a strong tradition that it's almost amazing that we've missed it.

- Jennifer Hecht

Doubters have been remarkably productive, for the obvious reason that they have a tendency toward investigation and, also, are often drawn to invest their own days with meaning.

- Jennifer Hecht

I'm sort of what I'll now call a Reagan atheist—came in real early. I was still a pretty young person.

- Jennifer Hecht

Good God, how much reverence can you have for a Supreme Being who finds it necessary to include such phenomena as phlegm and tooth-decay in His divine system of creation?

- Joseph Heller

Is not he Church to-day a masculine hierarchy, with a female constituency, which holds woman in Bible lands in silence and in subjection? No institution in modern civilization is so tyrannical and so unjust to woman as is the Christian Church. It demands everything from her and gives her nothing in return.

- Josephine K. Henry

Organized religion, which likes to fancy itself the mother of compassion, long ago lost its right to that claim by its organized support of organized cruelty.

- Jules Henry

I'm an atheist, and that's it. I believe there's nothing we can know except that we should be kind to each other and do what we can for each other.

- Katherine Hepburn

Now when I perceived that they [modern divines] resolved the causes of eternal salvation or damnation only to the good pleasure of God, and the death of Christ; I found that their opinion was grounded not on reason, but some peremptory decrees, which no body did pretend to know, and I could not think that they were so privy to the secret counsels of God, as to be able to establish any thing for certain; wherefore I left them, as entertaining mean, base, and unworthy thoughts of the most good and great God, and mankind in general.

- Edward Herbert

Our country has been hijacked by a bunch of religious nuts. But how easy it was. That's a little scary.

- Seymour Hersh

The atmosphere of piety in American public life has become stifling. Where is it written that if you don't like religion you are somehow disqualified from being a legitimate American? I'm pretty sure there is no such thing as god.

- Hendrik Hertzberg

Listen, the next revolution is gonna be a revolution of ideas. A bloodless revolution. And if I can take part in it by transforming my own consciousness, then someone else's, I'm happy to do it.

- Bill Hicks

The whole image is that eternal suffering awaits anyone who questions God's infinite love. That's the message we're brought up with, isn't it? Believe or die! Thank you, forgiving Lord, for all those options.

- Bill Hicks

You know, some people believe that they're Napoleon. That's fine. Beliefs are neat. Cherish them, but don't share them like they're the truth.

- Bill Hicks

I have to explain to people it was a joke. I'm an atheist.

- Peter Higgs

My body? Ah, if I could choose

I would to ashes it reduce,

And let the merry breezes blow

My dust to where some fading flowers grow.

Perhaps some fading flowers then

Would come to life and bloom again.

This is my last and final will.

Good luck to you.

- Joe Hill

Do you think I'm going to paradise? Of course not. I wouldn't go if I was asked. I don't want to live in some fucking celestial North Korea for one thing. Where all I get to do is praise the dear leader from dawn till dusk.

- Christopher Hitchens

The dullest mind can grasp . . . the deep connection between repression and perversion.

- Christopher Hitchens

Gullibility and credulity are considered undesirable qualities in every department of human life—except religion . . . Why are we praised by godly men for surrendering our 'godly gift' of reason when we cross their mental thresholds? . . . Atheism strikes me as morally superior, as well as intellectually superior, to religion. Since it is obviously inconceivable that all religions can be right, the most reasonable conclusion is that they are all wrong.

- Christopher Hitchens

If I was told to sacrifice (my children) to prove my devotion to God; if I was told to do what all monotheists are told to do and admire the man who said, 'Yes, I'll gut my kid to show my love to

God,' I'd say, 'No, fuck you!'

- Christopher Hitchens

Religion arouses suspicion by trying to prove too much.

- Christopher Hitchens

To hope to throw your sins on another, especially if this involves a human sacrifice, is a grotesque evasion of moral and individual responsibility.

- Christopher Hitchens

What can be asserted without proof can be dismissed without proof.

- Christopher Hitchens

I am now as before a Catholic and will always remain so.

- Adolf Hitler

My feeling as a Christian leads me to be a fighter for my Lord and Savior. It leads me to the man who, at one time lonely and with only a few followers, recognized the Jews for what they were, and called on men to fight against them. . . . As a Christian, I owe something to my own people.

- Adolf Hitler

Fear of power invisible, feigned by the mind or imagined from tales publicly allowed, *religion*; not allowed, *superstition*.

- Thomas Hobbes

Fear of things invisible is the natural seed of that which every one in himself calleth religion.

- Thomas Hobbes

Good and evil are names that signify our appetites and aversions.

- Thomas Hobbes

Seeing there are no signs nor fruit of religion but in man only, there is no cause to doubt but that the seed of religion is also only in man.

- Thomas Hobbes

They that approve a private opinion, call it opinion; but they that mislike it, heresy; and yet heresy signifies no more than private opinion.

- Thomas Hobbes

The facts on which the true believer bases his conclusions must not be derived from his experience or observation but from holy writ. . . . To rely on the evidence of the senses and of reason is heresy and treason. . . . Thus the effectiveness of a doctrine should not be judged by its profundity, sublimity or the validity of the truths it embodies, but by how thoroughly it insulates the individual from his self and the world as it is. What Pascal said of an effective religion is true of any effective doctrine: It must be 'contrary to nature, to common sense and to pleasure.'

- Eric Hoffer

A book that teaches the inferiority of women, the permissibility of slavery, the ostracism of non-Jews (and later, non-Christians), the stoning of disobedient sons, the necessity of blood-feud and vengeance, and a dozen other unsavory attitudes and rules, scarcely qualifies as an instrument of intellectual and social liberation.

- R. Joseph Hoffmann

When men have realized that time has upset many fighting faiths, they may come to believe even more than they believe the very foundations of their own conduct that the ultimate good desired is better reached by free trade in ideas—that the best test of truth is the power of the thought to get itself accepted in the competition of the market, and that truth is the only ground upon which their wishes can be carried out. That, at any rate, is the theory of our Constitution. It is an experiment, as all life is an experiment.

- Oliver Wendell Holmes Jr.

Free thought means fearless thought. It is not deterred by legal penalties, nor by spiritual consequences. Dissent from the Bible does not alarm the true investigator, who takes truth for authority not authority for truth. The thinker who is really free, is independent; he is under no dread; he yields to no menace; he is not dismayed by law, nor custom, nor pulpits, nor society—whose opinion appalls so many. He who has the manly passion of free thought, has no fear of anything, save the fear of terror.

- George Jacob Holyoake

By not believing in an afterlife it forces you to make the most out of this life to get the most out of the time you have.

- Alex Honnold

I was taken to church for maybe five or six years as a kid and at no point did I ever thing there was ever anything going on with church. I always saw it as a bunch of old people eating stale wafers, and that's totally weird to me.

- Alex Honnold

As a set of cognitive beliefs, religious doctrines constitute a speculative hypothesis of an extremely low order of probability.

- Sidney Hook

Where religion acquires institutional stability and authority, it is relatively indifferent to political freedom. . . . The religious view of the world becomes sensitive to human freedom only when it is being persecuted.

- Sidney Hook

Let God and man decree laws for themselves and not for me.

- A. E. Housman

The world can only be redeemed through action—movement—motion. Uncoerced, unbribed and unbought, humanity will move toward the light.

- Alice Hubbard

To talk about a Superior Being is a dip in superstition, and is just as bad as to let in an Inferior Being or a Devil. When you once attribute effects to the will of a personal God, you have let in a lot of little gods and evils—then sprites, fairies, dryads, naiads, witches, ghosts and goblins, for your imagination is reeling, riotous, drunk, afloat on the flotsam of superstition. What you know then doesn't count. You just believe, and the more you believe the more do you plume yourself that fear and faith are superior to science and seeing.

- Elbert Hubbard

As for those who protest that I am robbing people of the great comfort and consolation they gain from Christianity, I can only say that Christianity includes hell, eternal torture for the vast majority of humanity, for most of your relatives and friends. Christianity includes a devil who is really more powerful than God, and who keeps gathering into his furnaces most of the creatures whom God turns out and for whom he sent his son to the cross in vain. If I could feel that I have robbed anybody of his faith in hell, I should not be ashamed or regretful.

- Rupert Hughes

An intelligent hell would be better than a stupid paradise.

- Victor Hugo

Examine the religious principles which have, in fact, prevailed in the world, and you will scarcely be persuaded that they are anything but sick men's dreams.

- David Hume

No testimony is sufficient to establish a miracle, unless the testimony be of such a kind that its falsehood would be more miraculous than the fact that it endeavors to establish.

- David Hume

The Christian religion not only was at first attended with miracles, but even at this day cannot be believed by any reasonable person without one.

- David Hume

My head was full of misty fumes of doubt, . . . Neither could I understand the passionate declarations of love for a being that nobody could see. Your family, your puppy and the new bull-calf, yes. But a spirit away off who found fault with everybody all the time, that was more than I could fathom.

- Zora Neale Hurston

Strong, self-determining men are notorious for their lack of reverence. . . . Prayer seems to me a cry of weakness, and an attempt to avoid, by trickery, the rules of the game as laid down. I do not choose to admit weakness. I accept the challenge of responsibility. Life, as it is, does not frighten me, since I have made my peace with the universe as I find it, and bow to its laws. The ever-sleepless sea in its bed, crying out 'How long?' to Time; million-formed and never motionless flame; the contemplation of these two aspects alone, affords me sufficient food for ten spans of my expected lifetime. It seems to me that organized creeds are collections of words around a wish. I feel no need for such. However, I would not, by word or deed, attempt to deprive another of the consolation it affords. It is simply not for me. Somebody else may have my rapturous glance at the archangels. The springing of the yellow line of morning out of the misty deep of dawn, is glory enough for me. I know that nothing is destructible; things merely change forms. When the consciousness we know as life ceases, I know that I shall still be part and parcel of the world. I was a part before the sun rolled into shape and burst forth in the glory of change. I was, when the earth was hurled out from its fiery rim. I shall return with the earth to Father Sun, and still exist in substance when the sun has lost its fire, and disintegrated into infinity to perhaps become a part of the whirling rubble of space. Why fear? The stuff of my being is matter, ever changing, ever moving, but never lost; so what need of denominations and creeds to deny myself the comfort of all my fellow men? The wide belt of the universe has no need for finger-rings. I am one with the infinite and need no other assurance.

- Zora Neale Hurston

The world is not what I think but what I live.

- Edmund Husserl

Only humanism has a planetary perspective already in place. It is up to us to try to persuade the more open-minded members of the world community to join us in rejecting tribalism before it is too late.

- Duffy Hutcheon

Irrationality makes our lives make sense.

- Matthew Hutson

The past history of our globe must be explained by what can be seen to be happening now. No powers are to be employed that are not natural to the globe, no action to be admitted except those of which we know the principle.

- James Hutton

You shall know the truth and the truth shall make you mad.

- Aldous Huxley

I disbelieve in a personal God in any sense in which that phrase is ordinarily used. . . . I disbelieve in the existence of Heaven or Hell in any conventional Christian sense.

- Julian Huxley

Operationally, God is beginning to resemble not a ruler, but the last fading smile of a cosmic Cheshire cat.

- Julian Huxley

Blind faith, the one unpardonable sin.

- Thomas H. Huxley

In matters of the intellect, follow your reason as far as it will take you, without any other consideration. And negatively, in matters of the intellect, do not pretend that conclusions are certain which are not demonstrated or demonstrable.

- Thomas H. Huxley

Irrationally held truths may be more harmful than reasoned errors.

- Thomas H. Huxley

Skepticism is the highest duty and blind faith the one unpardonable sin.

- Thomas H. Huxley

The foundation of morality is to...give up pretending to believe that for which there is no evidence, and repeating unintelligible propositions, about things beyond the possibilities of knowledge.

- Thomas H. Huxley

# IBSEN

Bigger things than the State will fall, all religion will fall.

- Henrik Ibsen

I wish to say emphatically that there isn't a word of truth in this statement. Neither my sister nor myself is connected with any church in any way. Although our father has always wished for us to study and think for ourselves, we agree with him heartily in his religious belief.

- Maude Ingersoll

All religions are inconsistent with mental freedom. Shakespeare is my bible, Burns my hymn-book.

- Robert G. Ingersoll

By making a statute and by defining blasphemy, the church sought to prevent discussion.

- Robert G. Ingersoll

If a man would follow, today, the teachings of the Old Testament, he would be a criminal. If he would strictly follow the teachings of the New, he would be insane.

- Robert G. Ingersoll

The more false we destroy, the more room we make for the true.

- Robert G. Ingersoll

Tell them that they are my Holy Trinity comprising the only Deity I worship.

- Robert G. Ingersoll (about his wife and children)

With soap, baptism is a good thing.

- Robert G. Ingersoll

If you asked me another day, I'd just say flat out, 'No.'

- John Irving

Now, if you push me to the wall, I'd say I'm not a believer. But it depends on the day you ask. . . . I'm not comfortable calling myself a believer, a Christian. But if somebody says, 'are you an atheist?' I'd back down from that question too.

- John Irving

When you legislate personal belief, you're in violation of freedom of religion. The Catholic Church may espouse its opinion on abortion to the members of its congregation. But they are in violation of separation of church and state when they try to proselytize their abortion politics on people who are not Catholics.

- John Irving

# JAFFREE

I wanted to encourage toleration among my children. I certainly did not want teachers who have control over my children for least eight hours over the day to . . . program them into any religious philosophy.

- Ishmael Jaffree

If believing as though we have free will, or as if God exists, gets us the results we want, we will not only come to believe those things; they will be pragmatically true.

- William James

The world is all the richer for having a devil in it, so long as we keep our foot upon his neck.

- William James

And the day will come when the mystical generation of Jesus, by the supreme being as his father in the womb of a virgin, will be classed with the fable of the generation of Minerva in the brain of Jupiter.

- Thomas Jefferson

Because religious belief, or non-belief, is such an important part of every person's life, freedom of religion affects every individual. Religious institutions that use government power in support of themselves and force their views on persons of other faiths, or of no faith, undermine all our civil rights. Moreover, state support of an established religion tends to make the clergy unresponsive to their own people, and leads to corruption within religion itself. Erecting the 'wall of separation between church and state,' therefore, is absolutely essential in a free society.

- Thomas Jefferson

Christianity is the most perverted system that has ever shone upon man.

- Thomas Jefferson

Enlighten the people generally, and tyranny and oppressions of body and mind will vanish like evil spirits at the dawn of day.

- Thomas Jefferson

History, I believe, furnishes no example of a priest-ridden people maintaining a free civil government. This marks the lowest grade of ignorance of which civil as well as religious leaders will always avail themselves for their own purposes.

- Thomas Jefferson

I contemplate with sovereign reverence that act of the whole American people which declared that their legislature should make no law respecting an establishment of religion, or prohibit the free exercise thereof, thus building a wall of separation between church and state.

- Thomas Jefferson

Man, once surrendering his reason, has no remaining guard against absurdities the most monstrous, and like a ship without a rudder, is the sport of every wind. With such persons, which they call faith, takes the helm from the hand of reason and the mind becomes weak.

- Thomas Jefferson

Millions of innocent men, women, and children, since the introduction of Christianity, have been burnt, tortured, fined, and imprisoned; yet we have not advanced one inch toward uniformity. What has been the effect of coercion? To make one half the world fools and the other half hypocrites. To support roguery and error all over the earth.

- Thomas Jefferson

Question with boldness even the existence of a God; because, if there be one, he must more approve of the homage of reason than that of blindfolded fear. . . . Do not be frightened from this inquiry by any fear of its consequences. If it ends in a belief that there is no God, you will find inducements to virtue in the comfort and pleasantness you feel in its exercise, and the love for others which it will procure you.

- Thomas Jefferson

The [preachers] dread the advance of science as witches do the approach of daylight and scowl on the fatal harbinger announcing the subversions of the duperies on which they live.

- Thomas Jefferson

The greatest freedom you can enjoy is in obedience.

- Rulon Jeffs

Religious war? You're basically killing each other to see who's got the better imaginary friend.

- Richard Jeni

When one guy sees an invisible an he's a nut case. Ten people see him it's a cult. Ten million people see him it's a respected religion.

- Richard Jeni

I'm not a religious person. I would call myself an atheist. I don't have a good story behind it—I'm just reasonable.

- Anthony Jeselnik

Believing there is no God gives me more room for belief in family, people, love, truth, beauty, sex, Jell-O and all the other things I can prove and that make this life the best life I will ever have.

- Penn Jillette

Once you've condoned faith in general, you've condoned any crazy shit done because of faith.

- Penn Jillette

I am an atheist.

- Billy Joel

From my point of view, I would ban religion completely. The reality is that organized religion doesn't seem to work. It turns people into hateful lemmings and it's not really compassionate.

- Elton John

Religion has always tried to turn hatred toward gay people. Religion promotes the hatred and spite against gays.

- Elton John

I have to admit that one of my favorite fantasies is that next Sunday not one single woman, in any country of the world, will go to church. If women simply stop giving our time and energy to the institutions that oppress, they would have to cease to do so.

- Sonia Johnson

Yes, in fact I have. I have acquired the habit of free thought.

- Sonia Johnson

There doesn't need to be a God for me.

- Angelina Jolie

Ignorance is criminal.

- Scott Joplin

There is no harm in musical sounds. It matters not whether it is fast ragtime or a slow melody like 'The Rosary'.

- Scott Joplin

It is natural that people should differ most, and most violently, about the unknowable. . . . There is all the room in the world for divergence of opinion about something that, so far as we can realistically perceive, does not exist.

- E. Haldeman-Julius

# KAGIN

There are Atheists in foxholes

Atheists in hurricanes

There are Atheists in all the roles

Denied by your refrains

Atheists are your fellow citizens

People who love and laugh and cry

Atheists are your relatives and friends

Don't insult them with a lie

Atheists in many foxholes served

And some have had to die

Give Atheists the thanks deserved

Don't dismiss them with a lie

Atheists are all around you

They work, they help, they care

And no matter what you think is true

Atheists are everywhere

And no matter what you think is true

They do not want your prayer.

- Edwin Kagin

Atheists generate about as much sympathy as pedophiles. But, while pedophilia may at least be characterized as a disease, atheism is a choice, a willful rejection of beliefs to which vast majorities of people cling.

- Wendy Kaminer

I don't care if religious people consider me amoral because I lack their beliefs in God. I do, however, care deeply about efforts to turn religious beliefs into law, and those efforts benefit greatly from the conviction that individually and collectively, we cannot be good without God.

- Wendy Kaminer

The magical thinking encouraged by any belief in the supernatural, combined with the vilification of rationality and skepticism, is more conducive to conspiracy theories than it is to productive political debate.

- Wendy Kaminer

The church bells toll a melancholy round,

Calling the people to some other prayers,

Some other gloominess, more dreadful cares,

More hearkening to the sermon's horrid sound.

Surely the mind of man is closely bound

In some black spell; seeing that each one tears

Himself from fireside joys, and Lydian airs,

And converse high of these with glory crown'd.

Still, still they toll, and I should feel a damp,—

A chill as from a tomb, did I not know

That they are dying like an outburnt lamp;

That 'tis their sighing, wailing ere they go

Into oblivion;—that fresh flowers will grow,

And many glories of immortal stamp.

- John Keats

The most demoralizing factor in education is Christian religious instruction . . . even a more living, a more actual instruction in

Christianity injures the child. But the most dangerous of all educational mistakes in influencing humanity, is due to the fact, that children are now taught the Old Testament account of the world as absolute truth, although it wholly contradicts their physical and historical instruction. . . . But the demoralizing feature in Christianity as an ideal is, that it is presented as absolute, while man as a social being is obliged to transgress it every day. Besides he is taught in his religious instruction, that as a fallen being he cannot in any case attain the ideal, although the only possibility of his living righteously in temporal things, and happily in the world to come, depends on his capacity for realizing it.

- Ellen Key

Belief in myths allow the comfort of opinion without the discomfort of thought.

- John F. Kennedy

In the spring and with the coming of Easter, an old man's fancy lightly turns to thoughts of gods. I am now 83 pushing 84 and the closer I come to shuffling off this mortal coil, the more mystified I am by Christian belief in the deity they call by the not very original name of God (as if there had never been others). All gods from time immemorial are fantasies, created by humans for the welfare of humans and to attempt to explain the seemingly inexplicable. But do we, in the third year of the 21st century of the Common Era and on the springboard of colonizing the universe, need such palliatives? Wherever one looks there is conflict: Protestants and Catholics in Northern Ireland; Jews, Christians and Muslims in Palestine; Muslims and Hindus in the Indian subcontinent; Christians and Muslims in Nigeria, Indonesia, Saudi Arabia and elsewhere. Is not the case for atheism made?

- Ludovic Kennedy

If a doctor has a certain philosophic principle, religion or otherwise, that limits what he or she can do or say for the benefit of the patient, then he's not a full doctor. . . . A real doctor could divorce professional life from spiritual life.

- Jack Kevorkian

I never believed in god. I never believed in Santa Claus.

- Jack Kevorkian

Religion is telling law what to do, and law is telling doctors what to do. Religion dictates to law, and law dictates to ethics. No wonder we have problems. That's insanity!

- Jack Kevorkian

Women are made to be led, and counseled, and directed. . . . And if I am not a good man, I have no just right in this Church to a wife or wives, or the power to propagate my species. What then should be done with me? Make a eunuch of me, and stop my propagation.

- Heber C. Kimball

Privileged groups seldom give up their privilege voluntarily.

- Martin Luther King, Jr.

[James] Thurber had never allowed his probing, restless mind to settle on any single theological insurance policy concerning the possibilities of the hereafter. He remained an agnostic.

- Harrison Kinney

As a devout believer, [Gen.] Boykin may also wonder why it is impermissible to say that the God you believe in is superior to the God you don't believe in. I wonder this same thing as a nonbeliever: Doesn't one religion's gospel logically preclude the others'? (Except, of course, where they overlap with universal precepts, such as not murdering people, that even we nonbelievers can wrap our heads around.)

- Michael Kinsley

For a lot pf people, religion is the little lie that people believe, so they can believe the big lie of justice, mercy and fairness.

- Chris Kluwe

Universalists believe in a god which I do not; but believe that their god, with all his moral attributes, (aside from nature itself,) is nothing more than a chimera of their own imagination.

- Abner Kneeland

A fresh, cleansing wind swept through the stuffy room that contained the relics of my religious beliefs. I let them go with a profound sense of relief, and ever since I have lived happily without them.

- Margaret Knight

Combat the view that there can be no true morality without supernatural sanctions.

- Margaret Knight

Ethical teaching is weakened if it is tied up with dogmas that will not bear examination.

- Margaret Knight

I had been uneasy about religion throughout my adolescence, but I had not had the moral courage to throw off my beliefs until my third year in Cambridge.

- Margaret Knight

It is difficult . . . for the ordinary man to cast off orthodox beliefs, for he is seldom allowed to hear the other side. . . . Whereas the Christian view is pressed on him day in and day out.

- Margaret Knight

If only I wasn't an atheist. I could get away with anything. You'd just ask for forgiveness and then you'd be forgiven. It sounds much better than having to live with guilt.

- Keira Knightley

I had become an atheist at the age of thirteen, when atomic bombs were dropped on Japan.

- Paul Krassner

The amazing thing is that every atom in your body came from a star that exploded. And, the atoms in your left hand probably came from a different star than your right hand. It really is the most poetic thing I know about physics: You are all stardust. You couldn't be here if stars hadn't exploded, because the elements— the carbon, nitrogen, oxygen, iron, all the things that matter for evolution— weren't created at the beginning of time. They were created in the nuclear furnaces of stars, and the only way they could get into your body is if those stars were kind enough to explode. So, forget Jesus. The stars died so that you could be here today.

- Lawrence Krauss

The research data on distant, prayer-based healing are promising, but too sparse to allow any firm conclusion to be drawn.

- Stanley Krippner

The constant assertion of belief is an indication of fear.

- Jiddu Krishnamurti

There are serious problems confronting society and a 'humanitarian' God would not have allowed the unaccountable atrocities carried out in the name of any philosophy, religious or otherwise, to happen to anyone let alone to his/her/its chosen people. The desperate need we have for such organizations as Amnesty International has become, for me, one of the pieces of incontrovertible evidence that no divine (*mystical*) creator (other than the simple Laws of Nature) exists. . . . I am a devout atheist – nothing else makes any sense to me and I must admit to being bewildered by those, who in the face of what appears so obvious, still believe in a mystical creator.

- Harold Kroto

I was never a believer, but after seeing Czech Catholics persecuted during the Stalinist terror, I felt the deepest solidarity with them. What separated us, the belief in God, was secondary to what united us. In Prague, they hanged the Socialists and the priests. Thus a fraternity of the hanged was born.

- Milan Kundera

The Gospels are impaled on an irreconcilable contradiction.

- Paul Kurtz

The key to understanding who and what we are is that our futures, as individuals, societies or cultures, are not fixed or pre-ordained by some hidden hand of god; that what will become of us depends in part on what we choose to become.

- Paul Kurtz

We are not confined by our planet or solar system, but are capable of exploring galactic space. Our true identity is universal; we are not defined by the isms of the past, as Christian or Jew, Hindu or Muslim, nonbeliever or believer. Rather we are defined by our humanity.

- Paul Kurtz

I wrote the play in part out of my feeling as an agnostic. Huge questions about god emerge whenever a crisis the size of the AIDS epidemic or I think the political crisis of Reaganism appear on the scene. One begins to ask questions about the benevolence or presence of any kind of consciousness in the universe. I asked those questions—I was thinking a lot about death, I was thinking a lot about my own mortality, I was thinking a lot about justice and whether or not the world would resume what seemed to me a serious hampered progress towards something like social justice with someone like Reagan in the White House.

- Tony Kushner

# LA BRUVERE

To what excesses will men not go for the sake of a religion in which they believe so little and which they practice so imperfectly!

- Jean de La Bruyere

[The Catholic church] remains rooted in the past, an autocratic structure through which the pope and bishops make all decisions, and their constituents follow them without question.

- Lawrence Lader

[Robert] Ingersoll had a tremendous influence upon me, as indeed he had upon many young men of that time. It was not that he changed my beliefs, but that he liberated my mind. Freedom was what he preached: he wanted the shackles off everywhere. He wanted men to think boldly about all things: he demanded intellectual and moral courage. He wanted men to follow wherever truth might lead them. He was a rare, bold, heroic figure.

- Robert M. LaFollette, Sr.

If you believe in god and no god exists then your belief is an even greater wonder. Then it is really something inconceivably great. Why should a being lie down there in the darkness crying to someone who does not exist? Why should that be? There is no one who hears when someone cries in the darkness. But why does that cry exist?

- Pär Lagerkvist

All knowledge that is not the real product of observation, or of consequences deduced from observation, is entirely groundless and illusory.

- Jean Baptiste Lamarck

Mr. [Abraham] Lincoln was never a member of any Church, nor did he believe in the divinity of Christ, or the inspiration of the Scriptures in the sense understood by evangelical Christians. . . . When he came to New Salem, he consorted with Freethinkers, joined with them in deriding the gospel story of Jesus, read Volney and Paine, and then wrote a deliberate and labored essay, wherein he reached conclusions similar to theirs.

- Ward H. Lamon

The greatest difference between the Humanist ethic and that of Christianity and the traditional religions is that it is entirely based on happiness in this one and only life and not concerned with a realm of supernatural immortality and the glory of God. Humanism denies the philosophical and psychological dualism of soul and body and contends that a human being is a oneness of mind, personality, and physical organism. Christian insistence on the resurrection of the body and personal immortality has often cut the nerve of effective action here and now, and has led to the neglect of present human welfare and happiness.

- Corliss Lamont

Competition is as wholesome in religion as in commerce.

- Walter Savage Landor

Christianity may be good and Satanism evil. Under the Constitution, however, both are neutral.

- Kenneth V. Lanning

God is the greatest of man's inventions, and we are an inventive people, shaping the tools that in turn shape us, and we have at hand the technology to tell a new story congruent with the picture of the earth as seen from space instead of the one drawn on the maps available to the prophets wandering the roads of the early Roman Empire.

- Lewis Lapham

The dominant trait in the national character is the longing for transcendence and the belief in what isn't there—the promise of the sweet hereafter that sells subprime mortgages in Florida and corporate skyboxes in heaven.

- Lewis Lapham

Where there is doubt, there is freedom.

- Latin proverb

I'm not a religious man. Again, I think this is connected to my father. My father was religious oddly enough, but I nonetheless I suppose was impressed by [and] enamored of his devotion to medical science. I find I am a fan of science. I believe in science. A humility before the facts. I find that a moving and beautiful thing. And belief in the unknown I find less interesting. I find the known and the knowable interesting enough.

- Hugh Laurie

I was brought up an atheist and have always remained so. But at no time was I led to believe that morality was unimportant or that good and bad did not exist. I believe passionately in the need to distinguish between right and wrong and am somewhat confounded by being told I need God, Jesus or a clergyman to help me to do so.

- Nigella Lawson

I've been so relieved and so grateful to not have a god to believe in.

- Cloris Leachman

I came to be critical of formal religion, particularly of the damage that missionaries were doing to the culture of the people of Kenya. I had no difficulty in accepting the notion that standards of ethics and morality could be derived in the absence of religion. And I now believe that such standards are an inevitable—and predictable—product of human evolution.

- Richard Leakey

I didn't ever have religion.

- Richard Leakey

I myself do not believe in a god who has or had a human form and to whom I owe my existence. I believe it is man who created God in his image and not the other way round.

- Richard Leakey

I think 'intelligent design' is a rather shallow—and I would say unintelligent—attempt to pull wool over the eyes of the masses . . . you don't need to make something up when there is a perfectly good scientific explanation for life.

- Richard Leakey

Surely, [evolution] should be the pride and joy of African leaders. But the faith brigade, whether they're evangelical Christians, whether they're conservative Catholics, whether they're Islamic fundamentalists, are quite worried about this concept and are trying desperately to persuade ongoing future generations to have nothing to do with it. And in the process, [they] are putting people off science, putting people off the scientific method, putting people off the possibility of accepting facts.

- Richard Leakey

I rejected [Christianity] just after being 'confirmed' and told how essential it was to believe in all kinds of unbelievable things.

- Tim Berners-Lee

I am an atheist.

- Ursula K. Le Guin

If any of the three prongs of the Lemon Test are violated by an act of government, it is unconstitutional: 1) It must have a secular legislative purpose; 2) Its principal or primary effect must neither advance nor inhibit religion; 3) It must not foster excessive entanglement between government and religion.

- Alton Lemon

We're going back, back to the good old days,

When men were really men and women knew their place;

Back, back a couple of centuries,

And welcome back the days of the theocracy!

The family is so holy there must be no divorce.

And if a wife is not content, she must adjust, of course.

And if he's forced to beat her / it's all for her own good;

She must know what her limits are as any woman should!

- Kristin Lems

Religion is a kind of spiritual vodka in which the slaves of capital drown their human shapes and their claims to any decent human life.

- Vladimir Lenin

Christianity will go. It will vanish and shrink. I needn't argue about that. I'm right and I will be proved right. We are more popular than Jesus now. I don't know which will go first—rock and roll or Christianity. Jesus was all right, but his disciples were thick and ordinary. It's them twisting it that ruins it for me.

- John Lennon

God is a concept by which we can measure our pain.

- John Lennon

I don't believe in Bible.

- John Lennon

Imagine there's no heaven,

It's easy if you try,

No hell below us,

Above us only sky.

Imagine all the people

Living for today.

Imagine there's no country,

It isn't hard to do.

Nothing to kill or die for,

And no religion, too.

Imagine all the people

Living life in peace—

You may say I'm a dreamer.

But I'm not the only one.

I hope someday you'll join us,

And the world will be as one.

- John Lennon

This whole religion business suffers from the 'Onward, Christian Soldiers' bit. There's too much talk about soldiers and marching and converting. I'm not pushing Buddhism, because I'm no more a Buddhist than I am a Christian; but there's one thing I admire about the religion: There's no proselytizing.

- John Lennon

There are certain types of people who are political out of a kind of religious reason. I think it's fairly common among socialists: They are, in fact, God-seekers, looking for the kingdom of God on earth . . . If you don't believe in heaven, then you believe in socialism

- Doris Lessing

You'd never believe, when I was young, we genuinely believed religious wars were over. We'd say, at least it's impossible to have a religious war now. Can you believe that? . . . I'm so afraid of religion. Its capacity for murder is terrifying.

- Doris Lessing

Atheism rises above creeds and puts Humanity upon one plane. There can be no 'chosen people' in the Atheist philosophy. There are no bended knees in Atheism; No supplications, no prayers; No sacrificial redemptions; No 'divine' revelations; No washing in the blood of the lamb; No crusades, no massacres, no holy wars; No heaven, no hell, no purgatory; No silly rewards and no vindictive punishments; No christs, and no saviors; No devils, no ghosts and no gods.

- Joseph Lewis

It is, I think, an error to believe that there is any need of religion to make life seem worth living.

- Sinclair Lewis

When Fascism comes to America it will be wrapped in the flag and carrying a cross.

- Sinclair Lewis

What is to be, will be, and no prayers of ours can arrest the decree.

- Abraham Lincoln

I see no light behind that terrible curtain. I do not think one religion is better than another, and I think the Christian religion has brought far more misery, crime, and suffering, far more tyranny and evil, than any other.

- Eliza Lynn Linton

The radical novelty of modern science lies precisely in the rejection of the belief, which is at the heart of all popular religion, that the forces which move the stars and atoms are contingent upon the preferences of the human heart.

- Walter Lippmann

When men can no longer be theists, they must, if they are civilized, become humanists. Once you weaken the belief that the central facts taught by the churches are facts in the most literal and absolute sense, the disintegration of the popular religion begins.

- Walter Lippmann

It's irrational to fear what death will feel like if you know it won't feel like anything, but it doesn't follow that it is irrational to fear death. It's not irrational to look forward to the pleasures of living, and if we know that death will take these away, the fear of losing those pleasures doesn't seem irrational either.

- Peter Lipton

What a blessing to know there's a devil, and that I'm but a pawn in his game / that my impulse to sin doesn't come from within, and so I'm not exactly to blame.

- Frank Loesser

Brainwashed people do not know that they have been brainwashed.

- John W. Loftus

I'm not religious! I don't know if there's a God, but that's all I can say, honestly, is I don't know!

- Louis C. K.

A creed is the shell of a lie.

- Amy Lowell

Toward no crimes have men shown themselves so cold-bloodedly cruel as in punishing differences of belief.

- James Russell Lowell

I have little faith now, but I still look for truth, some momentary crumbling foothold.

- Robert Lowell

I should have no compassion on these witches; I should burn

them all.

- Martin Luther

Men have broad and large chests, and small narrow hips, and more understanding than women, who have but small and narrow breasts, and broad hips, to the end they should remain at home, sit still, keep house, and bear and bring up children.

- Martin Luther

No gown worse becomes a woman than the desire to be wise.

- Martin Luther

Reason is the greatest enemy that faith has: it never comes to the aid of spiritual things, but—more frequently than not—struggles against the Divine Word.

- Martin Luther

Reason must be deluded, blinded, and destroyed. Faith must trample underfoot all reason, sense, and understanding, and whatever it sees must be put out of sight and . . . know nothing but the word of God.

- Martin Luther

The word and works of God is quite clear, that women were made either to be wives or prostitutes.

- Martin Luther

To be a Christian, you must pluck out the eye of reason.

- Martin Luther

We are at fault for not slaying [the Jews].

- Martin Luther

We may well lie with what seems to be a woman of flesh and blood, and yet all the time it is only a devil in the shape of a woman.

- Martin Luther

The clergy, no less than the capitalist class, lives on the backs of the people, profits from the degradation, the ignorance and the oppression of the people.

- Rosa Luxemburg

# MACCREADY

[Humans are] a magnificent random experiment with no goal.

- Paul MacCready

I do not believe in God. I'm an atheist. I consider myself a critical thinker, and it fascinates me that in the 21st century most people still believe in, as George Carlin puts it, 'the invisible man living in the sky.'

- Seth MacFarlane

Over billions of years, on a unique sphere, chance has painted a thin covering of life—complex, improbable, wonderful and fragile. Suddenly we humans (a recently arrived species no longer subject to the checks and balances inherent in nature), have grown in population, technology, and intelligence to a position of terrible power: we now wield the paintbrush.

- Paul MacCready

The Christian religion, even now on its death bed, forges chains for the human race and continues to the last that hatred all knowledge and progressive improvement of mankind which has for a long time been one of its principal characteristics.

- William Maclure

The priests have retained their consideration and labor hard in their calling for the propagation of ignorance, superstition, and hypocrisy.

- William Maclure

The religious people are not with us. We believe they take exceptions to some of your writings, to the 8th article of our Constitution [prohibiting any religious instruction by members in the meeting] and to our meeting on a Sunday.

- William Maclure

We shall be astonished at the long continuance of the delusion that has led the human intellect astray, through the mysterious wilderness of deception, by the cunning intrigues of church and State.

- William Maclure

During almost fifteen centuries has the legal establishment of Christianity been on trial. What have been its fruits? More or less in all places, pride and indolence in the Clergy, ignorance and servility in the laity, in both, superstition, bigotry and persecution. . . . Torrents of blood have been spilt in the old world, by vain attempts of the secular arm, to extinguish Religious discord, by proscribing all difference in Religious opinion.

- James Madison

Religious bondage shackles and debilitates the mind and unfits it for every noble enterprise, every expanded prospect.

- James Madison

The civil government . . . functions with complete success . . . by the total separation of the Church from the State.

- James Madison

What influence, in fact, have ecclesiastical establishments had on society? In some instances they have been seen to erect a spiritual tyranny on the ruins of the civil authority; on many instances they have been seen upholding the thrones of political tyranny; in no instance have they been the guardians of the liberties of the people. Rulers who wish to subvert the public liberty may have found an established clergy convenient auxiliaries. A just government, instituted to secure and perpetuate it, needs them not.

- James Madison

Woman is a misbegotten man and has a faulty and defective nature in comparison to his. Therefore she is unsure in herself. What she cannot get, she seeks to obtain through lying and diabolical deceptions. And so, to put it briefly, one must be on one's guard with every woman, as if she were a poisonous snake and the horned devil. . . . Thus in evil and perverse doings woman is cleverer, that is, slyer, than man. Her feelings drive woman toward every evil, just as reason impels man toward all good.

- Albertus Magnus

I think flying planes into a building was a faith-based initiative. I think religion is a neurological disorder.

- Bill Maher

Religion must die for mankind to live.

- Bill Maher

When I hear from people that religion doesn't hurt anything, I say, really? Well besides wars, the Crusades, the Inquisitions, 9-11, ethnic cleansing, the suppression of women, the suppression of homosexuals, fatwas, honor killings, suicide bombings, arranged marriages to minors, human sacrifice, burning witches, and systematic sex with children, I have few quibbles. And I forgot about blowing up girl schools in Afghanistan.

- Bill Maher

After I had found nothingness, I found beauty.

- Stephane Mallarme

To the absurd myths of God and an immortal soul, the modern world in its radical impotence has only succeeded in opposing the ridiculous myths of science and progress.

- Andre Malraux

You would consider me an atheist or agnostic. I find religion and spirituality fascinating. I would like to believe this isn't the end and there's something more, but I can't convince the rational part of me that that makes any sense whatsoever.

- George R. R. Martin

My object in presenting the case against Christianity is

theoretical, not practical. I am not so naive as to suppose that the arguments set forth here will induce many people to give up their Christian beliefs. My claim that in light of my discussion rational people should give up these beliefs.

- Michael Martin

The lesson taught us by these kindly commentators on my present experience is that dogmatic faith compels the best minds and hearts to narrowness and insolence.

- Harriet Martineau

There is no theory of a God, of an author of Nature, of an origin of the Universe, which is not utterly repugnant to my faculties.

- Harriet Martineau

Religion is the sigh of the oppressed creature, the heart of a heartless world, and the soul of soulless conditions. It is the opium of the people.

- Karl Marx

The First requisite of the happiness of the people is the abolition of religion.

- Karl Marx

We need not take refuge in supernatural gods to explain our saints and sages and heroes and statesmen, as if to explain our disbelief that mere unaided human beings could be that good or wise.

- Abraham H. Maslow

Christianity pre-existed without the Personal Christ, that it was continued by Christians who entirely rejected the historical character in the Second Century, and that the supposed historic portraiture in the Canonical Gospels was extant as mythical and mystical before the Gospels themselves existed.

- Gerald Massey

Ever since there have been men, man has given himself over to

126

too little joy. That alone, my brothers, is our original sin. I should believe only in a God who understood how to dance.

- Henri Matisse

Hoping to God on high is like clinging to straws while drowning.

- Dave Matthews

I can't believe, in any way, in a god that cares about me. That makes no sense to me, a god that's watching me and hoping that I make the right choices. That god is impossible.

- Dave Matthews

I think God is more often a dangerous idea. . . . I think God is more often an excuse for not doing anything and more often an excuse for things that are wrong, to justify them. And that's not good.

- Dave Matthews

It would be safe to say that I'm agnostic.

- Dave Matthews

We owe a faith to the world and to ourselves. We owe a grace and gratitude to things that have brought us here. But I think it's very ignorant to say, 'Well, for everything, God has a plan.' That's like an excuse. Maybe the real faithful act is to commit to something, to take action, as opposed to saying, 'Well, everything is in the hand of God.'

- Dave Matthews

I do not believe in God. I see no need of such idea. It is incredible to me that there should be an afterlife. I find the notion of future punishment outrageous and of future reward extravagant. I am convinced that when I die, I shall cease entirely to live; I shall return to the earth I came from.

- W. Somerset Maugham

All that we find in Judaism and Christianity—there is virtually not one concept, belief, or idea expressed in Judaism or Christianity, not one—that cannot be traced back many, many times to many different religions. It's a very old, ancient story. It's the greatest story ever told.

- Jordan Maxwell

In his numerous historical and Scriptural works [Bruno] Bauer rejects all supernatural religion, and represents Christianity as a natural product of the mingling of the Stoic and Alexandrian philosophies.

- Joseph McCabe

I took a sheet of paper, divided it into debt and credit columns on the arguments for and against God and immortality. On Christmas Eve I wrote 'bankrupt' at the foot. And it was on Christmas morning 1895, after I had celebrated three Masses, while the bells of the parish church were ringing out the Christmas message of peace, that, with great pain, I found myself far out from the familiar land—homeless, aimlessly drifting. But the bells were right after all; from that hour on I have been wholly free from the nightmare of doubt that had lain on me for ten years.

- Joseph McCabe

Between being praised and persecuted, condoned and condemned, I might understandably have become bewildered, particularly at the brand of ethics sometimes displayed by the staunch defenders of Christianity. But of one thing I am sure: I am sure that I fought not only for what I earnestly believed to be right, but for the truest kind of religious freedom intended by the First Amendment, the complete separation of church and state.

- Vashi Cromwell McCollum

I am an atheist.

- Charlie McDonnell

I find that life is rich, diverse, fabulous, and extraordinary, conceived without a god.

- Ian McEwan

I'm an atheist. I really don't believe for a moment that our moral sense comes from a God . . . It's human, universal, [it's] being able to think our way into the minds of others . . . people who do not have a sky god and don't have a set of supernatural beliefs assert their belief in moral values and in love and in the transcendence that they might experience in landscape or art or music or sculpture or whatever. Since they do not believe in an afterlife, it makes them give more value to life itself. The little spark that we do have becomes all the more valuable when you can't be trading off any moments for eternity. . . . My own view of religion is that people must be free to worship all the gods they want. But it's only the secular spirit that will guarantee that freedom.

- Ian McEwan

Yes, I am an atheist, and probably Briony is, too. Atheists have as much conscience, possibly more, than people with deep religious conviction, and they still have the same problem of how they reconcile themselves to a bad deed in the past. It's a little easier if you've got a god to forgive you.

- Ian McEwan

I've often thought the Bible should have a disclaimer in the front saying this is fiction. I mean, walking on water, it takes an act of faith.

- Ian McKellen

The invisible and the non-existent look very much alike.

- Delos B. McKown

I'm an atheist and an anti-royalist, so why would I put anyone on a pedestal?

- Alexander McQueen

As my ancestors are free from slavery, I am free from the slavery of religion.

- Butterfly McQueen

At age fourteen I was asking questions. When the answers failed to satisfy me, I search elsewhere for different answers and found wisdom in atheism. And I am far from alone in that experience.

- Hemant Mehta

Backward and forward, eternity is the same; already we have been the nothing we dread to be.

- Herman Melville

Better sleep with a sober cannibal than a drunken Christian.

- Herman Melville

I believe that religion, generally speaking, has been a curse to mankind—that its modest and greatly overestimated services on the ethical side have been more than overcome by the damage it has done to clear and honest thinking. I believe that no discovery of fact, however trivial, can be wholly useless to the race, and that no trumpeting of falsehood, however virtuous in intent, can be anything but vicious. . . . I believe that the evidence for immortality is no better than the evidence of witches, and deserves no more respect. I believe in the complete freedom of thought and speech. . . . I believe in the capacity of man to conquer his world, and to find out what it is made of, and how it is run. I believe in the reality of progress. But the whole thing, after all, may be put very simply. I believe that it is better to tell the truth than to lie. I believe that it is better to be free than to be a slave. And I believe that it is better to know than be ignorant.

- H. L. Mencken

No one in this world, so far as I know . . . has ever lost money by underestimating the intelligence of the great masses of the plain people.

- H. L. Mencken

130

Puritanism - The haunting fear that someone, somewhere may be happy.

- H. L. Mencken

Sunday School: A prison in which children do penance for the evil conscience of their parents.

- H. L. Mencken

The chief contribution of Protestantism to human thought is its massive proof that God is a bore.

- H. L. Mencken

Theology: An effort to explain the unknowable by putting it into terms of the not worth knowing.

- H. L. Mencken

I do like talking with friends about big concepts, you know, the stuff that will ruin a party. To me, the party hasn't begun until we're talking about the nonexistence of God.

- James Mercer

There's no real reason for me to be so obsessed with trying to understand the true nature of things. You can live a perfectly happy life being utterly confused and not knowing.

- James Mercer

There was a half-assed attempt to give me religion. They sent me to a Catholic Sunday school . . . and they showed me videos of the end of the world. It seemed like a comic book and Satan was just another villain, like Lex Luthor or something. It seemed totally preposterous.

- James Mercer

The man who has no mind of his own lends it to the priests.

- George Meredith

When I was quite a boy, I had a spasm of religion which lasted six weeks . . . but I never since have swallowed the Christian fable.

- George Meredith

The only excuse for God is that he doesn't exist.

- Prosper Merimee

There are always, thank heaven, skeptics who challenge orthodox ideas. They are the great thinkers of all times.

- Barbara Mertz

I am a Humanist because I think humanity can, with constant moral guidance, create a reasonably decent society. I am terrified of restrictive religious doctrine, having learned from history that when men who adhere to any form of it are in control, common men like me are in peril. I do not believe that pure reason can solve the perceptual problems unless it is modified by poetry and art and social vision. So I am a humanist. And if you want to charge me with being the most virulent kind—a secular humanist—I accept the accusation.

- James Michener

My parents and grandparents—all of them Jews—went through huge trauma. They went through the trauma of the Holocaust. I don't know if it's for that reason that, by 1965, when I was born, my grandparents, who were alive, my parents were secular. But I've grown up in a secular way. I've thought about this, and I'm an atheist.

- David Miliband

I don't believe in god personally, but I have great respect for those people who do. Different people have different religious views in this country. The great thing is that, whether we have faith or not, we are by and large very tolerant of people whatever their view.

- Ed Miliband

The political climate in our house was generally and loosely left: it was unthinkable that a Jew, our sort of Jew, the artisan Jewish worker, self-employed, poor, Yiddish-speaking, unassimilated, non-religious, could be anything but socialistic.

- Ralph Miliband

I hope there are no religious services. . . . I would turn over in my grave.

- Harvey Milk (on his funeral)

The fact is that more people have been slaughtered in the name of religion than for any other single reason. That, that, my friends, that is true perversion!

- Harvey Milk

A large proportion of the noblest and most valuable teaching has been the work. not only of men who did not know, but of men who knew and rejected the Christian faith.

- John Stuart Mill

[Christianity is] essentially a doctrine of passive obedience; it inculcates submission to all authorities found established.

- John Stuart Mill

Every established fact which is too bad to admit of any other defense is always presented to us as an injunction of religion.

- John Stuart Mill

The Old Testament is responsible for more atheism, agnosticism, disbelief—call it what you will—than any book ever written; it has emptied more churches than all the counter-attractions of cinema, motor bicycle and golf course.

- A. A. Milne

And yes I have all of the usual objections

To the miseducation of children who, in tax-exempt institutions,

Are taught to externalize blame

And to feel ashamed and to judge things as plain right and wrong

But I quite like the songs.

- Tim Minchin

Passions, greed, hatred, and lies; social institutions, justice, love, glory, heroism, and religion: these are [the universe's] monstrous flowers and its hideous instruments of eternal human suffering.

- Octave Mirbeau

All religions are a deception of the people.

- Michael X. Mockus

I don't know nothing. Do you?

- Thelonious Monk

Man knows at last that he is alone in the universe's unfeeling immensity, out of which he emerged only by chance. His destiny is nowhere spelled out, nor is his duty. The kingdom above or the darkness below; it s for him to choose.

- Jacques Monod

Jane tried to convert me [to religion] and I tried to introduce her to Freud.

- Marilyn Monroe

The Good Book—one of the most remarkable euphemisms ever coined.

- Ashley Montagu

How many things served us yesterday for articles of faith, which today are fables to us?

- Michel de Montaigne

Man is certainly stark mad. He cannot make a flea, and yet he will be making gods by the dozen.

- Michel de Montaigne

Nothing is so firmly believed as what we least know.

- Michel de Montaigne

To know much is often the cause of doubting more.

- Michel de Montaigne

Women have never invented a religion; they are untainted with that madness, and they are not moralists.

- George Augustus Moore

Believing that we exist only in a single world, the natural world that we share with other living creatures, and that we have no special first-class tickets that allow for travel to continuous existence in other spheres at the end of our journey in this life. In our human distresses, we have only each other to turn to for help.

- Mary Morain

When Attorney General John Ashcroft repeatedly invokes religion, the Founders must be picketing in their graves. They were a mix of freethinkers, atheists, Christians, agnostics, Freemasons and Deists. . . . The Founders were, after all, revolutionaries. Their passion—especially regarding secularism— glows in the documents they forged and in their personal words.

- Robin Morgan

In Canada, you have fewer religious fanatics, there is much less violence in Canada and it's a much more tolerant society.

- Henry Morgentaler

Where it is a duty to worship the sun, it is pretty sure to be a crime to examine the laws of heat.

- John Morley

Salvation shall come from symbolism.

- Edvard Munch

My brief answer is that I am an atheist. . . . I'm not saying there isn't a god, but there isn't a god who cares about people. And who wants a god who doesn't give a shit?

- Robert Munsch

Christianity's history is rife with forgery and fraud. So rampant is this treachery and chicanery that any serious researcher must immediately begin to wonder about the story itself.

- D. M. Murdoch (Acharya S.)

The gospel story constitutes cultural bigotry and does a disservice to the history of humanity.

- D. M. Murdoch (Acharya S.)

There is not a single mention of Jesus by any historian contemporaneous with his alleged advent and . . . the biblical accounts are basically spurious, not written by their pretended authors, and riddled with tens of thousands of errors, impossibilities and contradictions.

- D. M. Murdoch (Acharya S.)

If you've got a religious belief that withers in the face of observations of the natural world, you ought to rethink your beliefs—rethinking the world isn't an option.

- P. Z. Myers

What I want to happen to religion in the future is this: I want it to be like bowling. It's a hobby, something some people will enjoy, that has some virtues to it, that will have its own institutions and its traditions and its own television programming, and that families will enjoy together. It's not something I want to ban or that should affect hiring and firing decisions, or that interferes with public policy. It will be perfectly harmless as long as we don't elect our politicians on the basis of their bowling score, or go to war with people who play nine-pin instead of ten-pin, or use folklore about backspin to make decrees about how biology works.

- P. Z. Myers

# NADAL

It's hard to say, 'I don't believe in God.' I would love to know if God exists. But it's a very difficult thing for me to believe. . . . I say, 'If God exists you don't need [to cross yourself] or pray.' If God exists, he's intelligent enough to [do] the important things, the right things.

- Rafael Nadal

The religion of one age is, as a rule, the literary entertainment of the next.

- Fridtjof Nansen

I am interested in this world, in this life, not in some other world or a future life.

- Jawaharlal Nehru

Every school morning in . . . public schools, government agents, teachers, funded with tax dollars, have their students stand up, including my daughter, face the flag of the United States of America, place their hands over their hearts, and affirm that ours is a nation under some particular religious entity, the appreciation of which is not accepted by numerous people, such as myself. We cannot in good conscience accept the idea that there exists a deity. I am an atheist. I don't believe in God. And every school morning my child is asked to stand up, face that flag, put her hand over her heart, and say that her father is wrong.

- Michael Newdow

And the Lord said:

I burn down your cities—how blind you must be.

I take from you your children and you say how blessed are we.

You all must be crazy to put your faith in me.

That's why I love mankind.

You really need me.

That's why I love mankind.

- Randy Newman

I grew up on the coast of England in the 70's. My dad is white from Cornwall and mum is black from Zimbabwe. Even the idea of us as a family was challenging to most people, but nature had its wicked way and brown babies were born. But, from about the age of five I was aware that I didn't fit, I was the black atheist kid in the all-white Catholic school run by nuns, I was an anomaly.

- Thandie Newton

I don't believe in God now.

- Jack Nicholson

There's an old saying that God exists in your search for him. I just want you to understand that I ain't looking.

- Leslie Nielsen

A church is something very beautiful. It is nice when people feel happy in it. But I am not a religious man. Look at us, and then at the infinity of space. We are rather small insignificant creatures, wouldn't you say?

- Oscar Niemeyer

After coming into contact with a religious man, I always feel I must wash my hands.

- Friedrich Nietszche

Christianity as antiquity.—When we hear the ancient bells growling on a Sunday morning we ask ourselves: Is it really possible! This, for a Jew, crucified two thousand years ago, who said he was God's son? The proof of such a claim is lacking. Certainly the Christian religion is an antiquity projected into our times from remote prehistory; and the fact that the claim is believed—whereas one is otherwise so strict in examining pretensions—is perhaps the most ancient piece of this heritage. A god who begets children with a mortal woman; a sage who bids men work no more, have no more courts, but look for the signs of the impending end of the world; a justice that accepts the innocent as a vicarious sacrifice; someone who orders his disciples to drink his blood; prayers for miraculous interventions; sins perpetrated against a god, atoned for by a god; fear of a beyond to which death is the portal; the form of the cross as a symbol in a time that no longer knows the function and ignominy of the cross—how ghoulishly all this touches us, as if from the tomb of a primeval past! Can one believe that such things are still believed?

- Friedrich Nietszche

Faith means not wanting to know what's true.

- Friedrich Nietszche

Great intellects are skeptical.

- Friedrich Nietszche

I beseech you, my brothers, remain faithful to the earth, and do not believe those who speak to you of otherworldly hopes!

- Friedrich Nietszche

One should not go to church if one wants to breathe pure air.

- Friedrich Nietszche

There is not sufficient love and goodness in the world to permit us to give some of it away to imaginary beings.

- Friedrich Nietszche

The Church is now more like the Scribes and Pharisees than like Christ. . . . What are now called the 'essential doctrines' of the Christian religion he does not even mention.

- Florence Nightingale

Shakespeare is my religion. Shakespeare has more wisdom and insight about our lives, about how to live and how not to live, how to forgive and how to understand our fellow creatures, than any religious tract. One hundred times more than the Bible.

- Trevor Nunn

I can stand at the beach's edge with the most devout Christian, Jew, Buddhist, go on down the line, and weep with the beauty of this universe and be moved by all of humanity. All the billions of people who have lived before us, who have loved and hurt and suffered. And so to me, my definition of God is humanity and is the love of humanity.

- Diana Nyad

# O'DOWD

For most of my life, I've been, 'Hey, I'm not into it, but I respect your right to believe whatever you want'. But as time goes on, weirdly, I'm growing less liberal. I'm more like, 'No, religion is ruining the world, you need to stop!'

- Chris O'Dowd

I have done that for years, looked up at it (the stars) and given it a wink and thought 'I don't know what's going on' and I still don't know what's going on, but I can't be consoled by mention of god. I can't. . . . And though I respect and adore the art that arises from the love of god and though nearly everybody I love and respect themselves believe in god, it is meaningless to me, really meaningless. . . . I have never believed in the Christian version of the individual creator.

- Nuala O'Faolain

When I'm dying, don't let a priest or Protestant minister or Salvation Army captain near me. Let me die in dignity. Keep it as simple and brief as possible. No fuss, no man of God there. If there is a God, I'll see him and we'll talk things over.

- Eugene O'Neill

I persist in preferring philosophers to rabbis, priests, imams, ayatollahs, and mullahs. Rather than trust their theological hocus-pocus, I prefer to draw on alternatives to the dominant philosophical historiography: the laughers, materialists, radicals, cynics, hedonists, atheists, sensualists, voluptuaries. They know that there is only one world, and that promotion of an afterlife deprives us of the enjoyment and benefit of the only one there is. A genuinely deadly sin.

- Michel Onfray

There is no such source and cause of strife, quarrel, fights, malignant opposition, persecution, and war, and all evil in the state as religion. Let it once enter our civil affairs, our government would soon be destroyed. Let it once enter our common schools, they would be destroyed. . . . Those who made our Constitution saw this, and used the most apt and comprehensive language in it to prevent such a catastrophe.

- Justice H. S. Orton

One must choose between God and Man, and all 'radicals' and 'progressives,' from the mildest liberal to the most extreme anarchist, have in effect chosen Man.

- George Orwell

My feelings on religion are starting to morph. I'm still very much an atheist, except that I don't necessarily see religion as a bad thing.... I'm almost saying certain people do better with religion, the way that certain rock stars do better if they're shooting heroin.

- Patton Oswalt

I am a retired Christian.

- Peter O'Toole

When did I realize I was God? Well, I was praying and I suddenly realized I was talking to myself.

- Peter O'Toole

Christianity is a formula: it is nothing more.

- Ouida

Finding that no religion is based on facts and cannot therefore be true, I began to reflect what must be the condition of mankind trained from infancy to believe in errors.

- Robert Owen

Relieve the human mind from useless and superstitious restraints.

- Robert Owen

# PACKER

Believe me, there is nothing on the other side. I've been there.

- Kerry Packer

The good news is there's no devil. The bad news is there's no heaven. There's nothing.

- Kerry Packer

All national institutions of churches, whether Jewish, Christian or Turkish, appear to me no other than human inventions, set up to terrify and enslave mankind, and monopolize power and profit.

- Thomas Paine

A man is preached instead of a God; an execution as an object for gratitude; the preachers daub themselves with the blood like a troop of assassins and pretend to admire the brilliancy it gives them. They preach a hum-drum sermon on being executed; and condemn the Jesus for doing it.

- Thomas Paine

Belief in a cruel god makes a cruel man.

- Thomas Paine

Is it more probable that nature should go out of her course, or that a man should tell a lie?

- Thomas Paine

It is a contradiction in terms and ideas to call any thing a revelation that comes to us second hand.

- Thomas Paine

Society is produced by our wants, and government by our wickedness; the former promotes our happiness positively by uniting our affections, the latter negatively by restraining our vices.

- Thomas Paine

That some desperate wenches should be willing to steal and enslave men by violence and murder for gain, is rather lamentable than strange. But that many civilized, nay, Christianized people should approve, and be concerned in the savage practice, is surprising.

- Thomas Paine

Whenever we read the obscene stories, the voluptuous debaucheries, the cruel and tortuous executions, the unrelenting vindictiveness, with which more than half the Bible is filled it would be more consistent that we call it the word of a demon than the word of God. It is a history of wickedness that has served to corrupt and brutalize.

- Thomas Paine

With respect to what are called denominations of religion, if every one is left to judge of his own religion, there is no such thing as a religion that is wrong; but if they are to judge of each others' religion, there is no such thing as a religion that is right; and therefore, all the world are right, or all the world are wrong.

- Thomas Paine

Another important doctrine of the Christian religion, is the atonement supposed to have been made by the death and sufferings of the pretended Saviour of the world; and this is grounded upon principles as regardless of justice as the doctrine o original sin. It exhibits a spectacle truly distressing to the feelings of the benevolent mind, it calls innocence and virtue into a scene of suffering, and reputed guilt, in order to destroy the injurious effects of real vice. It pretends to free the world from the fatal effects of a primary apostasy, by the sacrifice of an innocent being. Evil has already been introduced into the world, and in order to remove it, a fresh accumulation of crimes becomes necessary. In plain terms, to destroy one evil, another must be committed.

144

- Elihu Palmer

I'm at the atheist end of the agnostic spectrum.

- Sara Paretsky

It is amazing to me how quickly people can be stirred to behave in really vile ways, even though they may most of the time be warm and loving and decent people.

- Sara Paretsky

We'd be so hypocritical against our own thoughts if we said, ok, well let's not make fun of them [Muslims], because they might hurt us, like, that's messed up to have that kind of a thought process. OK, we'll rip on the Catholics because they won't hurt us, but we won't rip on them because they might hurt us.

- Trey Parker

Men never commit evil so fully and joyfully as when they do it for religious convictions.

- Blaise Pascal

Talking to god is crazy. Hearing god is schizophrenia. Acting on it is insanity.

- Robert Patterson

It is sometimes said that science has nothing to do with morality. This is wrong. Science is the search for truth, the effort to understand the world; it involves the rejection of bias, of dogma, of revelation, but not the rejection of morality.

- Linus Pauling

Humans saved themselves by creating religion, which enabled them to maintain themselves somehow, to survive in the midst of an uncompromising, all-powerful nature. It is a very basic instinct that is thoroughly rooted in human nature.

- Ivan Pavlov

In regard to my religiosity, my belief in God, my church

attendance, there is no truth in it; it is sheer fantasy.

- Ivan Pavlov

I was a seminarian, and like the majority of seminarians, I became an unbeliever, an atheist in my school years.

- Ivan Pavlov

There are weak people over whom religion has power. The strong ones–yes, the strong ones–can become thorough rationalists, relying only upon knowledge, but the weak ones are unable to do this.

- Ivan Pavlov

I believe that complete separation of church and state is one of those miraculous things which can be best for religion and best for the state, and the best for those who are religious and those who are not religious. I believe that the history of the First Amendment and also the Constitution itself, which forbids religious tests for public office, have testified to the healthful endurance of a principle which is the greatest treasure the United States has given the world: the principle of complete separation of church and state. I'm here to tell you that that principle is endangered today.

- Leo Pfeffer

There are religions which are not based on the existence of a personal deity.

- Leo Pfeffer

When I was a kid I used to pray every night for a new bicycle. Then I realized that the lord doesn't work that way so I stole one and asked him to forgive me.

- Emo Philips

Theologically speaking, Rod was what we call a naturalistic humanist, and that was the underlying philosophy of my pulpit. Racial issues, class, power—you find all of these in his writings, and he found reinforcements for his viewpoints in his congregation.

- Ernest Pipes

I don't believe in god. I don't believe in an afterlife. I don't believe in soul. I don't believe in anything. I think it's totally right for people to have their own beliefs if it makes them happy, but to me it's a pretty preposterous idea.

- Joaquin Phoenix

I'm not into organized religion. . . . For me, I believe in a God of whatever my own thing is.

- Joaquin Phoenix

The Methodist Discipline provides for 'separate Colored Conferences.' The Episcopal church shuts out some of its own most worthy ministers from clerical recognition, on account of their color. Nearly all denominations of religionists have either a written or unwritten law to the same effect. In Boston, even, there are Evangelical churches whose pews are positively forbidden by corporate mandate from being sold to any but 'respectable white persons.' Our incorporated cemeteries are often, if not always, deeded in the same manner. Even our humblest village grave yards generally have either a 'negro corner,' or refuse colored corpses altogether; and did our power extend to heaven or hell, we should have complexional salvation and colored damnation.

- Parker Pillsbury

Atheists are the most reviled minority in the United States, so it's no small matter to come out and say it. . . . I would put faith in the same category [as alchemy] because faith is believing something without a good reason to believe it.

- Steven Pinkler

I was never religious in the theological sense. I never outgrew my conversion to atheist at 13.

- Steven Pinkler

Universities are about reason, pure and simple. Faith—believing something without good reasons to do so—has no place in anything but a religious institution, and our society has no shortage of these. Imagine if we had a requirement for 'Astronomy and Astrology' or 'Psychology and Parapsychology'.

- Steven Pinkler

Virtually no scientist takes 'intelligent design' seriously, and in the famous Dover, Pa, trial in 2005, a federal court ruled that it is religion in disguise.

- Steven Pinkler

You know, I had my bar mitzvah when I was thirteen and I never entered a synagogue again. I've been to one or two marriages, I think, but I've never had anything to do with it.

- Harold Pinter

A person isn't considered insane if there are a number of people who believe the same way. Insanity isn't supposed to be a communicable disease. If one other person starts to believe him, maybe two or three, then it's a religion.

- Robert M. Pirsig

Religious mysticism is intellectual garbage. It's a vestige of the old superstitious Dark Ages when nobody knew anything and the whole world was sinking deeper and deeper into filth and disease and poverty and ignorance. It is one of those delusions that isn't called insane only because there are so many people involved.

- Robert M. Pirsig

When one person suffers from a delusion, it is called insanity. When many people suffer from a delusion it is called Religion.

- Robert M. Pirsig

I don't have a chance [on being elected Mayor of New Orleans]. I'm running on the gay marriage, no religion, legalization and taxation of marijuana platform.

- Brad Pitt

I'm probably 20 percent atheist and 80 percent agnostic.

- Brad Pitt

When I got untethered from the comfort of religion, it wasn't a loss of faith for me. It was a discovery of self. I had thought that I'm capable enough to handle any situation. There's peace in understanding that I have only one life, here and now, and I'm responsible.

- Brad Pitt

The only true divinity is humanity.

- William Pitt

How do you convince someone they're not thinking clearly, when they're not thinking clearly? What we're actually saying is no magic, no afterlife, no higher moral authoritative father-figure, no security, and no happy ever after. This is a tough sell.

- Phil Plait

The Universe is cool enough without making up crap about it.

- Phil Plait

I believe that this problem of theodicy, of understanding God's ways in the light of the mixture of goodness and terror which we find in the world, constitutes the greatest difficulty that people have in accepting a theistic view of reality. For those of us who stand within the Christian tradition, it remains a deep and disturbing mystery, nagging within us, of which we can never be unaware.

- John Polkinghorne

The question is, will the rest of America get fed up with fundamentalists before the fundamentalists and the Republican party get fed up with each other? And how much damage will they do before that happy day arrives?

- Katha Pollitt

You'd think by now politicians would realize that promoting family values is like wearing a Kick Me sign on your back.

- Katha Pollitt

I'm much more like the product of a doctor than I am a Jew. I don't believe in [an afterlife]. I believe this is it, and I believe it's the best way to live.

- Natalie Portman

No. I didn't have a bat mitzvah. And we never belonged to a temple. We felt it was ostentatious to belong to a temple.

- Natalie Portman

I'm an atheist. The good news about atheists is that we have no mandate to convert anyone. So you'll never find me on your doorstep on a Saturday morning with a big smile, saying, 'Just stopped by to tell you there is no word. I brought along this little blank book I was hoping you could take a look at.'

- Paula Poundstone

There is no God. At least, I'm practically certain there isn't. I don't believe there's a heaven or a hell either.

- Paula Poundstone

I read the Old Testament all the way through when I was about 13 and was horrified.

- Terry Pratchett

There is a rumor going around that I have found God. I think this is unlikely because I have enough difficulty finding my keys, and there is empirical evidence that they exist.

- Terry Pratchett

It is much to be lamented that a man of Dr. Franklin's general good character and great influence, should have been an unbeliever in Christianity, and also have done so much as he did to make others unbelievers.

- Joseph Priestley

The views I now entertain on such subjects as the plurality of worlds, cosmic evolution, the supervision and control of the universe, the infinities amid which we are placed, and so forth, are altogether unlike those which I indicated in my 'Other Worlds than Ours,' and others of my earlier works.

- Richard Proctor

At home we didn't talk about religion. So, gradually the question faded away by itself and disappeared from the agenda. When I was nineteen, my father died; my response to his death was atheistic.

- Sergei Prokofiev

When the faithful believe that they are worshiping . . ., they are in fact worshiping the standards of the clan itself.

- Marcel Proust

Every single religion that has a monotheistic god ends up by persecuting other people and killing them because they don't accept him. Wherever you look in history, you find that. It's still going on.

- Philip Pullman

I don't profess any religion; I don't think it's possible that there is a God; I have the greatest difficulty in understanding what is meant by the words 'spiritual' or 'spirituality.'

- Philip Pullman

When you look at what C.S. Lewis is saying, his message is so anti-life, so cruel, so unjust. The view that the *Narnia* books have for the material world is one of almost undisguised contempt. At one point, the old professor says, 'It's all in Plato'—meaning that the physical world we see around us is the crude, shabby, imperfect, second-rate copy of something much better. I want to emphasize the simple physical truth of things, the absolute primacy of the material life, rather than the spiritual or the afterlife.

- Philip Pullman

The last superstition of the human mind is the superstition that religion in itself is a good thing, though it might be free from dogma. I believe, however, that the religious feeling, as feeling, is wrong, and the civilized man will have nothing to do with it. . . . [When the] shadow of religion disappeared forever . . . I felt that I was free from a disease.

- Samuel Porter Putnam

# RADCLIFFE

I don't [believe in God]. I have a problem with religion or anything else that says, 'We have all the answers,' because there's no such thing as 'the answers.' We're complex. We change our minds on issues all the time. Religion leaves no room for human complexity.

- Daniel Radcliffe

Sweep aside those hatred-eaten mystics, who pose as friends of humanity and preach that the highest virtue man can practice is to hold his own life as of no value.

- Ayn Rand

I wish I believed I'd see my parents again, see my wife again. But I know its not going to happen.

- Tony Randall

We have fought long and hard to escape from medieval superstition. I, for one, do not wish to go back.

- James Randi

Fortunately I was brought up in a family in which religion played almost no part whatsoever.

- David Randolph

Faith will made, religions will flower and vanish, but reason remains.

- Ron Reagan

I'm sure there are all sorts of higher powers like electromagnetism and gravity, and things like that. But I don't believe in a deity, no. I see no evidence for that in my life or anywhere else in the universe.

- Ron Reagan

I would be unelectable; I'm an atheist. As we all know, that is something people don't accept.

- Ron Reagan

I tried to pray but I didn't feel any better, nor did I make any kind of connection with God.

- Christopher Reeve

It's frightening to me, the organized religion.

- Christopher Reeve

My father was not religious at all, so I really did not bother with questions of faith and spirituality.

- Christopher Reeve

The name of Christ has caused more persecutions, wars, and miseries than any other name has caused. The darkest wrongs are still inspired by it.

- John E. Remsburg

What happens when a students asks, 'Wait, how is salvation supposed to work? God came to Earth to sacrifice himself—to himself—to save humanity from being punished—by himself?' Pity the teachers stuck in this impossible spot.

- Scott Rhode

A religious person is a dangerous person. He may not become a thief or a murderer, but he is liable to become a nuisance. He carries with him many foolish and harmful superstitions, and he is possessed with the notion that it is his duty to give these superstitions to others. That is what makes trouble. Nothing is so worthless as superstition.

- Marilla M. Ricker

To affirm 'God does not exist', I do not have to hide behind Don Ignacio Ramírez; I am an atheist and I consider religions to be a form of collective neurosis. I am not an enemy of the Catholics,

154

as I am not an enemy of the tuberculars, the myopic or the paralytics; you cannot be an enemy of the sick, only their good friend in order to help them cure themselves.

- Diego Rivera

Soul is not even that Crackerjack prize that God and Satan scuffle over after the worms have all licked our bones. That's why, when we ponder—as sooner or later each of must—exactly what we ought to be doing about our soul, religion is the wrong, if conventional, place to turn. Religion is little more than a transaction in which troubled people trade their souls for temporary and wholly illusionary psychological comfort—the old give-it-up-in-order-to-save-it routine. Religions lead us to believe that the soul is the ultimate family jewel and that in return for our mindless obedience, they can secure it for us in their vaults, or at least insure it against fire and theft. They are mistaken.

- Tom Robbins

I agree with Francis Crick, the eminent Cambridge don, the winner of the Nobel Prize for his co-discovery of the double helix, the blueprint of life, who wrote: 'In the fullness of time, educated people will believe there is no soul independent of the body, and hence no life after death.'

- Chalmers Roberts

I do want to add a final word about the hereafter. I do not believe in it. I think that the religions which promise various after-life scenarios basically invented them to meet the longing for an answer to life's mysteries.

- Chalmers Roberts

I contend that we are both atheists. I just believe in one fewer god than you do. When you understand why you dismiss all the other possible gods, you will understand why I dismiss yours.

- Stephen Roberts

Petronius was surely right in saying *Fear made the gods*. In primitive times fear of *the* unknown was normal; gratitude to *an* unknown was impossible.

- J. M. Robertson

The feminist agenda is not about equal rights for women. It is about a socialist, anti-family political movement that encourages women to leave their husbands, kill their children, practice witchcraft, destroy capitalism and become lesbians.

- Pat Robertson

I have always been reasonably leery of religion because there are so many edicts in religion, 'thou shalt not,' or 'thou shalt.' I wanted my world of the future to be clear of that.

- Gene Roddenberry

[Inspiration's] a bad word for what happens to me when I write. What I do is not as fancy as some people may think. . . . This isn't a question of sitting on the top of a hill and waiting for inspiration to strike. It's work. People have said 'You're a genius.' I say, 'No, it's my job.'

- Richard Rodgers

I disagree with manipulative approaches to therapy; to assume that one person can be in charge of another's life is a dangerous philosophy. My own philosophy is based on the conviction that people have within themselves the resources and capacity for self-understanding and self-correction. . . . In the [Northern Ireland encounter] groups, you see each other as a person, not as those evil Catholics and Protestants. The feelings of irrational hostility dissolve.

- Carl Rogers

In the theory of evolution there is no talk of God and no Bibles are used. They're not looking for higher powers, extraterrestrials, or anything else that could be found in the science fiction section, because they are not dealing with fiction.

- Henry Rollins

Everyone has the right to freedom of thought, conscience and religion; this right includes freedom to change his religion or belief.

- Eleanor Roosevelt

The Bible illustrated by Dore occupied many of my hours—and I think probably gave me many nightmares.

- Eleanor Roosevelt

[I am] a decided skeptic. . . . Professed no religious faith and practiced no regular religious observances.

- Dante Gabriel Rossetti

Man is born free; and everywhere he is in chains.

- Jean Jacques Rousseau

Whoever dares to say: 'Outside the Church is no salvation,' ought to be driven from the State. But I am mistaken in speaking of a Christian republic; the terms are mutually exclusive. Christianity preaches only servitude and dependence. Its spirit is so favorable to tyranny that it always profits by such a regime. True Christians are made to be slaves, and they know it and do not much mind: this short life counts for too little in their eyes.

- Jean Jacques Rousseau

Yes, I believe in revelation, but a permanent revelation of man to himself and by himself, a rational revelation that is nothing but the result of the progress of science and of the contemporary conscience, a revelation that is always only partial and relative and that is effectuated by the acquisition of new truths and even more by the elimination of ancient errors. We must also attest that the progress of truth gives us as much to forget as to learn, and we learn to negate and to doubt as often as to affirm.

- Clemence Royer

I'm a nonbeliever. I don't believe in the existence of a God. I don't believe in the Christian dogma. I find it horrifyingly silly. The intolerance that flows from organized religion is the most dangerous thing on the planet.

- Jane Rule

If the moderate voices of Islam cannot or will not insist on the modernization of their culture—and of their faith as well—then it may be these so-called 'Rushdies' who have to do it for them. For every such individual who is vilified and oppressed, two more, ten more, a thousand more will spring up. They will spring up because you can't keep people's minds, feelings and needs in jail forever, no matter how brutal your inquisitions.

- Salman Rushdie

In India, as elsewhere in our darkening world, religion is the poison in the blood. Where religion intervenes, mere innocence is no excuse. Yet we go on skating around this issue, speaking of religion in the fashionable language of 'respect.' What is there to respect in any of this, or in any of the crimes now being committed almost daily around the world in religion's dreaded name?

- Salman Rushdie

The idea of the sacred is quite simply one of the most conservative notions in any culture, because it seeks to turn other ideas—uncertainty, progress, change—into crimes.

- Salman Rushdie

Where there is no belief, there is no blasphemy.

- Salman Rushdie

It is neither Madonna-worship nor saint-worship, but the evangelical self-worship and hell-worship—gloating, with an imagination as unfounded as it is foul, over the torments of the damned, instead of the glories of the blest—which have in reality degraded the languid powers of Christianity to their present state of shame and reproach.

158

- John Ruskin

A good world needs knowledge, kindliness, and courage; it does not need a regretful hankering after the past, or a fettering of the free intelligence by the words uttered long ago by ignorant men.

- Bertrand Russell

As soon as we abandon our own reason, and are content to rely upon authority, there is no end to our troubles.

- Bertrand Russell

Cruel men believe in a cruel God and use their belief to excuse their cruelty. Only kindly men believe in a kindly God, and they would be kindly in any case.

- Bertrand Russell

I believe that when I die I shall rot, and nothing of my ego will survive. I am not young, and I love life. But I should scorn to shiver with terror at the thought of annihilation. Happiness is nonetheless true happiness because it must come to an end, not do thought and love lose their value because they are not everlasting.

- Bertrand Russell

I see no reason whatsoever to believe in immortality.

- Bertrand Russell

My own view on religion is that of Lucretius. I regard it as a disease born of fear and as a source of untold misery to the human race.

- Bertrand Russell

One of the most interesting and harmful delusions to which men and nations can be subjected is that of imagining themselves special instruments of the Divine Will.

- Bertrand Russell

# SACKETT

I am a Humanist and a freethinker because, as Mr. Spock would say, it is only logical.

- Susan Sackett

A universe with no edge in space, no beginning or end in time, and nothing for a creator to do.

- Carl Sagan

If some good evidence for life after death were announced, I'd be eager to examine it; but it would have to be real scientific data, not mere anecdote. As with the face on Mars and alien abductions, better the hard truth, I say, than the comforting fantasy. And in the final tolling it often turns out that the facts are more comforting than the fantasy.

- Carl Sagan

Not only is there no evidence that a lack of religiosity leads to less moral behavior, a number of studies actually support the opposite view.

- Carl Sagan

I have always been an atheist. My parents were atheists. It doesn't bother me if somebody is religious. My problem is when religion is used to institutionalize other things.

- Lakshmi Sahgal

To work hard, to live hard, to die hard, and then to go to Hell after all would be too damned hard.

- Carl Sandburg

About the holy book, I tend to say: read the Bible and you'll lose your faith.

- José Saramago

All religions, without exception, have done humanity more bad than good.

- José Saramago

God only exists in our minds.

- José Saramago

Christianity persecuted, tortured, and burned. Like a hound it tracked the very scent of heresy. It kindled wars, and nursed furious hatreds and ambitions. It sanctified, quite like Mohammedanism, extermination and tyranny.

- George Santayana

My atheism, like that of Spinoza, is true piety toward the universe and denies only gods fashioned by men in their own image, to be servants of their human interests.

- George Santayana

No religion has ever given a picture of deity which men could have imitated without the grossest immorality.

- George Santayana

That fear first created the gods is perhaps as true as anything so brief could be on so great a subject.

- George Santayana

The fact of having been born is a bad augury for immortality.

- George Santayana

We should have to abandon our vested illusions, our irrational religions and patriotisms.

- George Santayana

What religion a man shall have is a historical accident, quite as much as what language he shall speak.

- George Santayana

The Old Testament's full of good stories, my personal favorites being those of David and Esther. I never could get into the New Testament.

- Pamela Sargent

We have lost religion, but we have gained humanism.

- Jean-Paul Sartre

I'm actually the fourth generation in my family to have no practical use for the church, or God, or religion. My children continue this trend.

- Adam Savage

The idea of an ordered and elegant universe is a lovely one. One worth clinging to. But you don't need religion to appreciate the ordered existence. It's not just an idea. It's reality. We're discovering the hidden orders of the universe every day. The inverse square law of gravitation is amazing. Fractals, the theory of relativity, the genome: these are magnificently beautiful constructs.

- Adam Savage

Ignore the bullshit in the bible about gay people.

- Dan Savage

My father was a Catholic deacon, my mother was a lay minister and I thought about becoming a priest. I was in church every Sunday for the first 15 years of my life. Now I spend my Sundays on my bike, on my snowboard or on my husband. I haven't spent my post-Catholic decades in a sulk, wishing the church would come around on the issue of homosexuality so that I could start attending Mass again. I didn't abandon my faith. I saw through it. The conflict between my faith and my sexuality set that process in motion, but the conclusions I reached at the end of that process—there are no gods, religion is man-made, faith can be a force for good or evil—improved my life. I'm grateful that my sexuality prompted me to think critically about faith. Pushed out? No. I walked out.

- Dan Savage

As a historian, I confess to a certain amusement when I hear the Judeo-Christian tradition praised as the source of our concern for human rights. In fact, the great religious ages were notable for their indifference to human rights in the contemporary sense. They were notorious not only for acquiescence in poverty, inequality, exploitation and oppression but for enthusiastic justifications of slavery, persecution, abandonment of small children, torture, genocide.

- Arthur Schlesinger, Jr.

In view of the tide of religiosity engulfing a once secular republic, it is refreshing to be reminded by *Freethinkers* that free thought and skepticism are robustly in the American tradition. After all, the Founding Fathers began by omitting God from the American Constitution.

- Arthur Schlesinger, Jr.

Public prayer is not intended to promote religious values, but to enhance the authority of some churches and some political views over others. Similarly with the posting of the Ten Commandments. It is about power, not about religion. Government by Christian or Islamic or any other faith has rarely been progressive. And the Constitution clearly intends that there should be freedom from religion.

- Ellery Schempp

All religions promise a reward for excellences of the will or heart, but none for excellences of the head or understanding.

- Arthur Schopenhauer

Faith and knowledge are related as the two scales of balance; when the one goes up, the other goes down. . . . The power of religious dogma, when inculcated early, is such as to stifle conscience, compassion, and finally every feeling of humanity. . .

. For, as you know, religions are like glow worms; they shine only when it's dark. A certain amount of ignorance is the condition of all religions, the element in which alone they can exist.

- Arthur Schopenhaur

But we, wretched unbelievers, we bear our own burdens; we must say, 'I myself did it, I. Not God, not Satan; I myself!'

- Olive Schreiner

This thing is certain—he is a fool who says, 'No man hath said in his heart, There is no God.'

- Olive Schreiner

The freethinker has the same right to discredit the beliefs of Christians that the Orthodox Christians enjoy in destroying reverence, respect, and confidence in Mohammedanism, Mormonism, Christian Science, or Atheism.

- Theodore Schroedor

The best theology is probably no theology; just love one another.

- Charles Schulz

On the available evidence we have about how the world works, we have to say that we're alone, there is no God.

- John Searle

I feel most spiritual when I'm out in the woods. I feel part of nature. Or looking up at the stars. [I used to say] I was an atheist. Now I say, it's all according to your definition of God.

- Pete Seeger

I leaf through [the Bible] quite often—if only to shake my head in disgust. I quote Leviticus to people who think that every word in the Bible is absolutely gospel and you need to obey every word. In Leviticus it says you must kill a bull if you're going to really love God. And you must kill it in a certain way, or else you will be killed.

- Pete Seeger

[Georg] Buchner, in the brief span of his life, manifested much of that spirit of Thomas Paine which stalked through Germany during centuries, which has thrust into the flesh of theology the thorn of higher criticism.

- George Seibel

And so [my brother] Gilbert and I, brought up without a formal religion, remained throughout our lifetimes just what Father was, freethinkers. And, likewise, doubters and dissenters and perhaps Utopians. Father's rule had been 'Question everything, take nothing for granted,' and I never outlived it, and I would suggest it be made the motto of a world journalists' association.

- George Seldes

I never yet have seen the person who could withstand the doubt and unbelief that enter his mind when reading the Bible in a spirit of inquiry.

- Etta Semple

I'm not unhappy about becoming old. I'm not unhappy about what must be. It makes me cry only when I see my friends go before me and life is emptied . . . It's harder for us nonbelievers.

- Maurice Sendak

[Albert Camus'] anti-Christianity is one of the most absolute of modern times.

- Martin Seymour-Smith

In religion, what damned error but some sober brow will blest it, and approve it with a text . . . ?

- William Shakespeare

Of God, the Devil and Darwin, we have really good scientific evidence for the existence of only Darwin.

- Niall Shanks

It is not disbelief that is dangerous to society, it is belief.

- George Bernard Shaw

Personally, I prefer the garden to the cloister.

- George Bernard Shaw

The fact that a believer is happier than a skeptic is no more to the point than the fact that a drunken man is happier than a sober one.

- George Bernard Shaw

There is nothing in religion but fiction.

- George Bernard Shaw

Whether Socrates got as much out of life as Wesley [John Wesley, founder of Methodism] is an unanswerable question, but a nation of Socrateses would be much safer and happier than a nation of Wesleys.

- George Bernard Shaw

If ignorance of nature gave birth to gods, knowledge of nature is made for their destruction.

- Percy Bysshe Shelley

It is among men of genius and science that atheism alone is found.

- Percy Bysshe Shelley

Oh, that the wise from their bright minds would kindle such lamps within the dome of this dim world, that the pale name of priest might shrink and dwindle into the Hell from which it first was furled.

- Percy Bysshe Shelley

Smart people believe weird things because they are skilled at defending beliefs they arrived at for non-smart reasons.

- Michael Shermer

I can sum up the philosophical conception of my new work in three words: life is beautiful. . . . Everything that is dark and gloomy will rot away, vanish, and the beautiful will triumph.

- Dmitriy Shostakovich

The greatest contribution nonbelievers have made to the world has been the Constitution of the United States. Consider how very heretical to a religious world was the idea of a Constitution predicated on 'We, the People.'

- Queen Silver

I'm so associated with being Jewish—and I do it myself—but I have no religion. . . . I wasn't raised with any religion, I have no religion.

- Sarah Silverman

Sell the Vatican, take a big chunk of that money, build a gorgeous condominium for you and all of your friends to live in, all the amenities, swimming pool, tennis court, water slide. And with the money left over, feed the whole fucking world. You preach to live humbly, and I totally agree. So now maybe it's time for you to move out of your house that is a city.

- Sarah Silverman

Yes, I'm agnostic. I don't know. I just don't know. I think people need religion because they need to know. They need to get their head around it. But you know, I don't know. I don't know what the answers are.

- Sarah Silverman

I got no religion in me. I could never see through it. Basically, I'm a facts man; if I can't see through it, I say it's not possible. In my lifetime, I bet you we killed thirty to forty million people. It's dictators. It's religion. But we've got that stopped, I'm sure. I'd say the atomic bomb stopped everybody short.

- J. R. Simplot

You're dead, that's the end of you. There's no tomorrow.

- J. R. Simplot

There are a score of great religions in the world . . . and each is a mighty fortress of graft.

- Upton Sinclair

Let us see how steadfast I am. One of my friends asked me to pray. When informed of my atheism, he said, 'When your last days come, you will begin to believe.' I said, 'No, dear sir, Never shall it happen. I consider it to be an act of degradation and demoralization. For such petty selfish motives, I shall never pray.' Reader and friends, is it vanity? If it is, I stand for it.

- Bhagat Singh

For tens of thousands of years, humans have stared up into the heavens and wondered about the origin of the universe. Up until now every culture, society, and religion has had nothing else to turn to except its creation myths, fables, or religious scriptures. Today, by contrast, we have the extraordinary privilege of being the first generation of our species to have access to a scientific theory of the universe that explains its origin and evolution.

- Simon Singh

My Grandmother Skinner made sure that I understood the concept of hell by showing me the glowing bed of coals in the parlor stove. In a traveling magician's show I saw a devil complete with horns and barbed tail, and I lay awake all that night in an agony of fear. Miss Graves [a teacher], though a devout Christian, was liberal. She explained, for example, that one might interpret the miracles in the Bible as figures of speech. . . . Within a year I had gone to Miss Graves to tell her that I no longer believed in God. 'I know,' she said, 'I have been through that myself.' But her strategy misfired: I never went through it.

- B. F. Skinner

If evolution were not a real phenomenon, then fields like genetic

168

engineering . . . would not even exist!

- Ardea Skybreak

When a mere girl, my mother offered me a dollar if I would read the Bible through; . . . despairing of reconciling many of its absurd statements with even my childish philosophy, . . . I became a skeptic, doubter, and unbeliever, long ere the 'Good Book' was ended.

- Elmina D. Slenker

Science is the great antidote to the poison of enthusiasm and superstition.

- Adam Smith

Virtue is more to be feared than vice, because its excesses are not subject to the regulation of conscience.

- Adam Smith

The root of masculine is stronger, and of feminine weaker. The sun is a governing planet to certain planets, while the moon borrows her light from the sun, and is less or weaker.

- Joseph Smith

The tragedy is that every brain cell devoted to belief in the supernatural is a brain cell one cannot use to make life richer or easier or happier.

- Kay Nolte Smith

This is what made me an atheist. Consider how deeply witch craze was rooted in religion. The papal sanction was not abolished for six centuries. How can anyone belong to a church that treated its members this way?

- Kay Nolte Smith

I recently read *The God Delusion* by Richard Dawkins, which ignited my interest in a scientific, mathematical version of the world. No, I'm not religious. At all. I'm an atheist.

- Matt Smith

Were there atheists in foxholes during World War II? Of course, as can be verified by my dog tags. . . . A veteran of Omaha Beach in 1944, I insisted upon including 'None' instead of P, C, or J as my religious affiliation.

- Warren Allen Smith

For the first time the earth had a provable history, a written record that paid no heed or obeisance to religious teaching and dogma, that declared its independence from the kind of faith that is no more than the blind acceptance of absurdity. A science . . . had now at last broken free from the age-old constraints of doctrine and canonical instruction.

- William Smith

People who believe in a divine creator, trying to live their lives in obedience to his supposed wishes and in expectation of a supposed eternal reward, are victims of the greatest confidence trick of all time.

- Barbara Smoker

I feel that religion, adopted purely, is ultimately representative of blindly making someone else's beliefs your own.

- Edward Snowden

Nothing with gods, nothing with fate;

Weighty affairs will just have to wait!

Nothing that's formal,

Nothing that's normal,

No recitations to recite;

Open up the curtain:

Comedy Tonight!

- Stephen Sondheim

We have our religious fanatics fighting their religious fanatics, which leaves me without a side to root for.

- Edward Sorel

Superstition is the tyranny of tyrannies, and its priests the tyrants of tyrants.

- Charles Southwell

Prosperity theology elevates greed to a virtue instead of leaving it as one of the seven deadly sins.

- DeForest Souries

Religion has been compelled by science to give up one after another of its dogmas, of those assumed cognitions which it could not substantiate.

- Herbert Spencer

How blest would our age be if it could witness a religion freed from all the trammels of superstition!

- Benedict Spinoza

I do not know how to teach philosophy without becoming a disturber of established religion.

- Benedict Spinoza

Philosophy has no end in view save truth; faith looks for nothing but obedience and piety.

- Benedict Spinoza

[Sin] cannot be conceived in a natural state, but only in a civil state, where it is decreed by common consent what is good or bad.

- Benedict Spinoza

The most tyrannical governments are those which make crimes of opinions, for everyone has an inalienable right to his thoughts.

- Benedict Spinoza

Those who wish to seek out the causes of miracles, and to understand the things of nature as philosophers, and not to stare at them in astonishment like fools, are soon considered heretical and impious, and proclaimed as the interpreters of nature and the gods.

- Benedict Spinoza

True virtue is life under the direction of reason.

- Benedict Spinoza

We can always get along better by reason and love of truth than by worry of conscience and remorse.

- Benedict Spinoza

After a lot of reading, and research, I realized, I didn't have any secret channel picking up secret messages from god or anyone else. That voice in my head was my own.

- Greydon Square

I think we have an excess of faith-based initiatives in recent years.

- Richard Stallman

Religious people often say that religion offers absolute certainty about right and wrong; 'god tells them' what it is. Even supposing that the aforementioned gods exist, and that the believers really know what the gods think, that still does not provide certainty, because any being no matter how powerful can still be wrong. Whether gods exist or not, there is no way to get absolute certainty about ethics. Without absolute certainty, what do we do? We do the best we can. Injustice is happening now; suffering is happening now. We have choices to make now. To insist on absolute certainty before starting to apply ethics to life decisions is a way of choosing to be amoral.

- Richard Stallman

Embrace truth as it is revealed today by human reason.

- Elizabeth Cady Stanton

I have endeavoured to dissipate these religious superstitions from the minds of women, and base their faith on science and reason, where I found for myself at least that peace and comfort I could never find in the Bible and the church . . . the less they believe, the better for their own happiness and development. . . . For fifty years the women of this nation have tried to dam up this deadly stream that poisons all their lives, but thus far they have lacked the insight or courage to follow it back to its source and there strike the blow at the fountain of all tyranny, religious superstition, priestly power, and the canon law.

- Elizabeth Cady Stanton

In the early days of woman-suffrage agitation, I saw that the greatest obstacle we had to overcome was the bible. It was hurled at us on every side.

- Elizabeth Cady Stanton

The Church is a terrible engine of oppression, especially as concerns woman.

- Elizabeth Cady Stanton

The memory of my own suffering has prevented me from ever shadowing one young soul with the superstitions of the Christian religion.

- Elizabeth Cady Stanton

You may go over the world and you will find that every form of religion which has breathed upon this earth has degraded woman.

- Elizabeth Cady Stanton

It's not courageous to make a simple statement about personal beliefs. What is courageous is to stand up in Congress and say, 'Let's tax the rich and give the money to poor kids'.

- Pete Stark

Like our nation's founders, I strongly support the separation of church and state. I look forward to working with the Secular

Coalition to stop the promotion of narrow religious beliefs in science, marriage contracts, the military and the provision of social services.

- Pete Stark

Thankfully, we're moving in a direction where some feel it's not an act of courage simply to state that you don't believe in god. The work of the Freedom From Religion Foundation is helping to make this possible.

- Pete Stark

That's all religion is—some principle you believe in . . . man has accomplished far more miracles than the God he invented. What a tragedy it is to invent a God and then suffer to keep him King.

- Rod Steiger

Now finally, I am not religious so that I have no apprehension of a hereafter, either a hope or reward or a fear of punishment. It is not a matter of belief. It is what I feel to be true from my experience, observation, and simple tissue feeling.

- John Steinbeck

We have usurped many of the powers we once ascribed to God. Fearful and unprepared, we have assumed lordship over the life or death of the whole world—of all living things. The danger and the glory and the choice rest finally in man. The test of his perfectibility is at hand. Having taken Godlike power, we must seek in ourselves for the responsibility and the wisdom we once prayed some deity might have. Man himself has become our greatest hazard and our only hope. So that today, St. John the apostle may well be paraphrased: In the end is the Word, and the Word is Man—and the Word is with Men.

- John Steinbeck

It's an incredible con job, when you think of it, to believe something now in exchange for life after death. Even corporations, with all their reward systems, don't try to make it posthumous.

- Gloria Steinem

Modern science finds no evidence to support revelation as a source of information, no sign of intelligent design, and no need for everything to have a cause. It is likely that the multiverse is eternal, with no beginning, no end, and no need of a creator.

- Victor Stenger

Religion is an intellectual and moral sickness that cannot endure forever if we believe at all in human progress.

- Victor Stenger

I now believe in nothing, to put it shortly; but I do not the less believe in morality.

- Leslie Stephen

I want you to know I read EVERY WORD of *Freethought Today*. When my copy arrives I feel as if I have received a love letter.

- Irene Stephenson

To be happy, you have to be what is natural for you, not what someone else wants you to be.

- Irene Stephenson

I don't believe in God.

- Bruce Sterling

Some people recognized the moral perils of mixing religion and politics, . . . but many more were seduced by it. It was the pseudo-religious transfiguration of politics that largely ensured [Hitler's] success, notably in Protestant areas.

- Fritz Stern

After one has abandoned a belief in God, poetry is the essence which takes its place as life's redemption.

- Wallace Stevens

I am religious in my own way, but I am hardly brave enough to interpose a theory of my own between life and death. Here both our creeds and our philosophies seem to me to fail.

- Robert Louis Stevenson

I believe in you as others believe in the Bible.

- Robert Louis Stevenson

Under the wide and starry sky

Dig the grave and let me lie.

Glad did I live and gladly die,

And I laid me down with a will.

This be the verse you 'grave for me:

Here he lies where he long'd to be;

Home is the sailor, home from the sea,

And the hunter home from the hill.

- Robert Louis Stevenson

If ever I'm asked if I'm religious I always reply, 'Yes, I'm a devout musician.' Music puts me in touch with something beyond the intellect, something otherworldly, something sacred.

- Sting

Do not think that I am jesting or speaking figuratively when I regard those persons who cling to the Higher, and (because the vast majority belongs under this head) almost the whole world of men, as veritable fools, fools in a madhouse.

- Max Stirner (Johann Kaspar Schmidt)

Religion itself is without genius. There is no religious genius, and no one would be permitted to distinguish between the talented and the untalented in religion.

- Max Stirner (Johann Kaspar Schmidt)

The religious spirit is not inspired. Inspired piety is as great an inanity as inspired linen-weaving. Religion is always accessible to the impotent, and every uncreative dolt can and will always have religion, for uncreativeness does not impede his life of dependency.

- Max Stirner (Johann Kaspar Schmidt)

We are perfect altogether, and on the whole earth there is not one man who is a sinner! There are crazy people who imagine that they are God the Father, God the Son, or the man in the moon, and so too the world swarms with fools who seem to themselves to be sinners; but, as the former are not the man in the moon, so the latter are not sinners. Their sin is imaginary.

- Max Stirner (Johann Kaspar Schmidt)

We're atheists who don't hate religion, who are kind of fascinated by it and kind of admire it.

- Matt Stone

I see children forced to attend church school and Hebrew school and they hate it, they don't fall back on it in tough times. When they are 15 and start asking more questions they will have to come to that conclusion themselves.

- John Stossel

I want evidence. I want reason and explanation . . . I like to report on what I know, what I've researched and understand.

- John Stossel

I fear that parliament may set up a little state church to make people morally good . . . it will make them immoral, for it will inaugurate bitterness and ill feeling.

- Robert Stout

We recognize no authority competent to dictate to us. Each must believe what he considers to be true and act up to his belief, granting the same right to everyone else.

- Robert Stout

Some of these televangelists have taken advantage of the fact that churches have little regulation by government and few reporting requirements.

- Paul Streckfus

I follow no doctrine. I don't belong to a church or a temple or a synagogue or an ashram.

- Meryl Streep

I grudgingly went to Sunday Hebrew school, but mostly, I think, we were sent just to get us out of the house. . . . We were not what you would call religious, and this has stuck with me to this day.

- Charles Strouse

My sister died in '41 of breast cancer, and I remember a rabbi saying that 'God in his infinite wisdom has chosen to take this young girl.' That was a point in my life that I said there couldn't be any God.

- Charles Strouse

Do I believe in any god or gods or supernatural destiny? No. I'm an atheist from way back. If you believe there is some god or gods watching over you, more power to you and your imagination. From Thomas Edison to Albert Einstein, the most knowledgeable scientists of our time—and those who best understood how the universe works—discarded the idea of a personal deity.

- Lyle Stuart

I receive too many emails from women in the Islamic world, telling me: 'Go ahead, we are behind you,' but unfortunately they're afraid for their lives.

- Wafa Sultan

It took me years, but letting go of religion has been the most profound wake up of my life. I feel I now look at the world not as a child, but as an adult. I see what's bad and it's really bad. But I also see what is beautiful, what is wonderful. And I feel so deeply appreciative that I am alive. How dare the religious use the term 'born again.' That truly describes freethinkers who've thrown off the shackles of religion so much better!

- Julia Sweeney

Why isn't there a book about someone losing their faith and it being this beautiful experience?

- Julia Sweeney

I believe in nature instead of God.

- Matthew Sweet

If you talk to God, you are praying. If God talks to you, you have schizophrenia.

- Thomas Szasz

# TAYLOR

Twelve-step programs say an interesting thing; Either you have a god, or you are God and you don't want the job.

- James Taylor

Well, I find myself with a strong spiritual need—in the past five years, particularly. And, certainly, it's acknowledged as an important part of recovery from addiction. Yet it's hard for me to find an actual handle for it. I'm not saying that it's not helpful to think of having a real handle on the universe, your own personal point of attachment. But . . . I think it's crazy. But it's an intensity that keeps us sane. You might call a lot of these songs 'spirituals for agnostics.'

- James Taylor

When individuated consciousness comes up against the idea of individual death, something's got to give. That's why people invent afterlives, and versions of the afterlife, which there is absolutely no evidence for whatsoever. . . . I think God is the name of a question. God is not an existing thing.

- James Taylor

I have found some astonishing answers to my questioning as to God and religion in his book.

- Peter Ilyich Tchaikovsky

In our windy world, what's up is faith, what's down is heresy.

- Alfred Tennyson

I'm an agnostic. . . . I don't believe in any afterlife. I do believe in this life, and what do you do in this life is what it's all about.

- Louis Terkel

In pain shall you bring forth children, woman, and you shall turn to your husband and he shall rule over you. And do you not know that you are Eve? God's sentence hangs still over all your sex and His punishment weighs down upon you. You are the devil's gateway; you are she who first violated the forbidden tree and broke the law of God. It was you who coaxed your way around him whom the devil had not the force to attack. With what ease you shattered that image of God: Man! Because of the death you merited, even the Son of God had to die. . . . Woman, you are the gate to hell.

- Tertullian

Woman is a temple built over a sewer.

- Tertullian

If we go back to the beginning we shall find that ignorance and fear created the gods.

- Paul-Henri Thiry

Atheists pay taxes, too.

- Helen Thomas

Mr. President, why do you refuse to respect the wall between the church and the state? And you know that the mixing of religion and government for centuries has led to slaughter. I mean, the very fact that our country has stood in good stead by having the separation—why do you break it down? . . . Well, you wouldn't have a religious office in the White House if you did. . . . You are a secular official. And not a missionary.

- Helen Thomas

Secularism is spreading incredibly fast.

- Damian Thompson

I'm an atheist; I suppose you can call me a sort of libertarian anarchist. I regard religion with fear and suspicion. It's not enough to say that I don't believe in God. I actually regard the system as distressing: I am offended by some of the things said in the Bible and the Koran, and I refute them.

- Emma Thompson

I think that the Bible as a system of moral guidance in the 21st Century is insufficient. I feel quite strongly that we need a new moral lodestone if we can't rely on what is inside our own selves.

- Emma Thompson

It is better to know some of the questions than all of the answers.

- James Thurber

I'm not a practicing anything. I've been brought up around Buddhism and I'm very interested in it, and if I have any leaning I would lean toward Buddhist feelings. But as I have seen so many devout people, I wouldn't categorize myself as a practicing person.

- Uma Thurman

Hold your spiritual bromides . . . Pat [Tillman] isn't with God. He's f-ing dead. He wasn't religious. So thank you for your thoughts, but he's f-ing dead.

- Richard Tillman

Any incipient spirit of religion [Erich Maria Remarque] may have acquired during his schooldays was to be tested and found wanting by his experiences on the western front, evolving instead into a brand of humanism he worked out for himself.

- Hilton Tims

That not adhering to those notions Reason dictates (concerning the nature of God), has been the occasion of all superstition, and those innumerable mischiefs that mankind (on account of religion) have done to themselves or to one another.

- Matthew Tindal

Freethinkers are those who are willing to use their minds without prejudice and without fearing to understand things that clash with their customs, privileges, or beliefs. This state of mind is not common, but it is essential for right thinking; where it is absent, discussion is apt to become worse than useless.

- Leo Nikolaevich Tolstoi

If there is no higher reason—and there is none—then my own reason must be the supreme judge of my life.

- Leo Nikolaevich Tolstoi

One may say with one's lips: 'I believe that God is one, and also three'--but no one can believe it, because the words have no sense.

- Leo Nikolaevich Tolstoi

To regard Christ as God, and to pray to him, are to my mind the greatest possible sacrilege.

- Leo Nikolaevich Tolstoi

The point at issue is not whether I believe in a supreme being, but whether the state has a right to inquire into my beliefs.

- Roy Torcaso

I find it kind of distasteful having religions that tell you what you can do and what you can't do.

- Linus Torvalds

I find that people seem to think religion brings morals and appreciation of nature. I actually think it detracts from both . . . I think we can have morals without getting religion into it, and a lot of bad things have come from organized religion in particular. I actually fear organized religion because it usually leads to misuses of power.

- Linus Torvalds

In practice, religion has absolutely nothing to do with everyday life.

- Linus Torvalds

Whatever a man prays for, he prays for a miracle. Every prayer reduces itself to this: Great God, grant that twice two be not four.

- Ivan Turgenev

God has given an immortal soul to every man and woman, but not to any other animal or machine. Hence no animal or machine can think. I am unable to accept any part of this.

- Alan Turing

I am not very impressed with theological arguments whatever they may be used to support. Such arguments have often been found unsatisfactory in the past. In the time of Galileo it was argued with the texts, 'And the sun stood still ... and hasted not to go down about the whole day.' (Joshua x.13) and 'He laid the foundations of the earth, that it should not move at any time,' (Psalm cv.5) were an adequate refutation of the Copernican theory.

- Alan Turing

I think in my life I've never heard atheism put forward better than by Graham [Greene].

- Robin Turton

Faith is believing what you know ain't so.

- Mark Twain

Get your facts first, and then you can distort them as much as you please.

- Mark Twain

I cannot see how a man of any large degree of humorous perception can ever be religious—except he purposely shut the eyes of his mind & keep them shut by force.

- Mark Twain

It ain't those parts of the Bible that I can't understand that bother me, it is the parts that I do understand.

- Mark Twain

Man is the only religious animal. He is the only animal that has the True Religion—several of them. He is the only animal that loves his neighbor as himself and cuts his throat, if his theology isn't straight. He has made a graveyard of the globe in trying his honest best to smooth his brother's path to happiness and heaven.

- Mark Twain

The man with a new idea is a Crank until the idea succeeds.

- Mark Twain

There is no humor in heaven.

- Mark Twain

I don't want students who could make the next major breakthrough in renewable energy sources or space travel to have been taught that anything they don't understand, and that nobody yet understands, is divinely constructed and therefore beyond their intellectual capacity. The day that happens, Americans will just sit in awe of what we don't understand, while we watch the rest of the world boldly go where no mortal has gone before.

- Neil deGrasse Tyson

I have yet to see a successful prediction about the physical world that was inferred or extrapolated from the content of any religions document.

- Neil deGrasse Tyson

Intelligent design is a philosophy of ignorance. You cannot build a program of discovery on the assumption that nobody is smart enough to figure out the answer to a problem.

- Neil deGrasse Tyson

I think, based on all the folks who are agnostic historically, I come closer to the behavior of an agnostic than the behavior of an atheist.

- Neil deGrasse Tyson

Let there be no doubt that as they are currently practiced, there is no common ground between science and religion.

- Neil deGrasse Tyson

# UPDEGRAPH

The Holy Scriptures were a mere fable, that they were a contradiction, and that although they contained a number of good things, yet they contained a great many lies.

- Abner Updegraph

I'm offended by [evangelical leaders'] actions, but I'm not offended by their opinion. They believe in a sky god who's going to suck them up into the sky with a vacuum cleaner. What's there to get offended by? That's funny! That's hilarious! Have at it, Hoss, I'd love to see it!

- Cenk Uygur

# VAN BEETHOVAN

Man, help thyself.

- Ludwig van Beethovan

I would thank God, but I don't believe in it.

- Eddie Vedder

The planet was never threatened. How did they survive for all this time without this belief in God? I'd like to ask this to someone who knows about Christianity and maybe you do. That just seems funny to me.

- Eddie Vedder

The word 'religion' has such bad connotations for me, that it's been responsible for wars, and it shouldn't be that way at all, it's just the way the meaning of the word has evolved to me. I have to wonder what we did on this planet before religion.

- Eddie Vedder

When you're out in the desert, you can't believe the amount of stars. We've sent mechanisms out there, and they haven't found anything. They've found different colors of sand, and rings and gases, but nobody's shown me anything that makes me feel secure in what happens afterward. All I really believe in is this moment, like right now. And that, actually, is what the whole album [*Ten*] talks about.

- Eddie Vedder

For me, the lines between church and state seem to become more blurred by the day. The First Amendment protects freedom of speech, thought—*and* religion. Nowhere is it mandated that we're the Christian States of America. . . . That's made us, I think, a stronger and more democratic nation. . . . It's abundantly clear that our Founding Fathers wanted to prevent our government from establishing a 'national church'.

- Jesse Ventura

I was the only governor of all fifty who would not declare a National Day of Prayer. I took a lot of heat for that, and my response was very simple: Why do people need the government to tell them to pray? Pray all you want! Pray fifty times a day if you desire, it's not my business! . . . If I declare National Day of Prayer, then I've got to declare National No-Prayer Day for the atheists. They are American citizens too.

- Jesse Ventura

Organized religion is a sham and a crutch for the weak-minded people who need strength in numbers.

- Jesse Ventura

Stay away from priests.

- Giuseppe Verdi

Follow Nature's law.

- Theophile de Viau

Christianity is such a silly religion.

- Gore Vidal

I regard monotheism as the greatest disaster ever to befall the human race. I see no good in Judaism, Christianity, or Islam.

- Gore Vidal

The great unmentionable evil at the center of our culture is monotheism. From a barbaric Bronze Age text known as the Old Testament, three anti-human religions have evolved—Judaism, Christianity, and Islam. These are sky-god religions. They are, literally, patriarchal—God is the Omnipotent Father—hence the loathing of women for 2000 years in those countries afflicted by the sky-god and his earthly male delegates. The sky-god is a jealous god, of course. He requires total obedience from everyone on earth, as he is not just in place for one tribe, but for all creation. Those who would reject him must be converted or killed for their own good.

- Gore Vidal

[Thomas Gore] was a dedicated atheist. Imagine, he was senator for over thirty years in Oklahoma, a hotbed of the Lord Jesus, and they never found out.

- Gore Vidal

Atheism is the vice of a few intelligent people. There are no sects in geometry. The truths of religion are never so well understood as by those who have lost the power of reasoning. Sect and error are synonymous. Common sense is not so common.

- Voltaire

[A true god] surely cannot have been born of a girl, nor died on the gibbet, nor be eaten in a piece of dough . . . [or inspired] books, filled with contradictions, madness, and horror.

- Voltaire

But how conceive a God supremely good

Who heaps his favors on the sons he loves,

Yet scatters evil with as large a hand?

- Voltaire

Christianity is the most ridiculous, the most absurd, and bloody religion that has ever infected the world.

- Voltaire

My interest in believing something is not proof of its existence.

- Voltaire

The people receive religion and laws in the same way they receive coins: without examining them.

- Voltaire

190

During World War II, while I was serving with the Third Army in Germany, I removed a belt buckle from the uniform of a dead German soldier. The lettering on the buckle read *Gott Mit Uns* (God Is With Us).

- Kurt Vonnegut (in *Slaughterhouse Five*)

I am an atheist (or at best a Unitarian who winds up in churches quite a lot).

- Kurt Vonnegut

Which religion do I profess to follow? None! And why? Because of religion.

- Friedrich von Schiller

I can relate [to Spanish King Charles II's belief that the corpse of St. Francis of Assissi would cure his various illnesses]. . . . I crave my relics for the same reason Señor Bewitched bunked with the late saint. We're religious. I used to share the king's faith. And while I gave up God a long time ago, I never shook the habit of wanting to believe in something bigger and better than myself. So I replaced my creed of everlasting life with life, liberty and the pursuit of happiness. 'I believe in America,' chants the first verse of one of my sacred texts, The Godfather.'

- Sarah Vowell

# WALLAS

In the same way when we dream we draw absurd inferences by association. Even when men are awake, those parts of their mind to which for the moment they are not giving full attention are apt to draw equally unfounded inferences. People in a state of strong religious emotion sometimes become conscious of a throbbing sound in their ears, due to the increased force of their circulation. An organist, by opening the thirty-two foot pipe, can create the same sensation, and can thereby induce in the congregation a vague and half-conscious belief that they are experiencing religious emotion.

- Graham Wallas

It is chilling to think that the same people who persecuted the wise women and men of Europe, its midwives and healers, then crossed the oceans to Africa and the Americas and tortured and enslaved, raped, impoverished, and eradicated the peaceful, Christ-like people they found. And that the blueprint from which they worked, and still work, was the Bible.

- Alice Walker

Religious controversies are always productive of more acrimony and irreconcilable hatreds than those which spring from any other cause. Of all the monstrosities which have existed among mankind, those which are caused by difference of sentiment in religion appear to be the most inveterate and distressing, and ought most to b deprecated. I was in hopes that the enlightened and liberal policy which has marked the present age would at least have reconciled Christians of every denomination, so far that we should never again see their religious disputes carried to such a pitch as to endanger the peace of society.

- George Washington

I didn't ever smash up a hotel room or throw a TV out a window.

That was Led Zeppelin. Thank god. If there was a god, you know, which there isn't.

- Roger Waters

Through the power of money, And the power of your prayers, What God wants God gets God help us all. God wants dollars, God wants cents, God wants pounds shillings and pence . . . God don't want small potatoes, God wants small towns, God wants pain . . . God wants TV, God wants contributions, What God wants God gets God help us all. God wants silver, God wants gold, God wants his secret never to be told. God wants fame, God wants credit, God wants blame, God wants poverty, God wants wealth, God wants insurance, God wants to cover himself. What God wants God gets God help us all.

- Roger Waters

I am happy that I can aid those admirable men, both living and dead, who by their pens or their tongues have aided the great cause of human liberty and universal happiness.

- James Watson

Every time you understand something, religion becomes less likely. Only with the discovery of the double helix and the ensuing genetic revolution have we had grounds for thinking that the powers held traditionally to be the exclusive property of the gods might one day be ours. . . . [As a young man] I came to the conclusion that the church was just a bunch of fascists that supported Franco. I stopped going on Sunday mornings and watched the birds with my father instead.

- James D. Watson

A few saints and a little charity don't make up for all the harm religion has done over the ages.

- Peter Watson

I lead a perfectly healthy, satisfactory life without being religious. And I think more people should try it.

- Peter Watson

Religion has kept civilization back for hundreds of years, and the biggest mistake in the history of civilization, is ethical monotheism, the concept of the one God. Let's get rid of it and be rational.

- Peter Watson

If Christianity contained any real remedy for existing evils, it would have displayed itself ere now. It has had every advantage in its favor; the influence of the priests, the patronage of kings, the alliance of the great and powerful, the use of untold wealth, the command of the armies, first place among the councilors of nations, the willing subjection of the populace. . . . It has been absolute monarch of the world. Yet with all these advantages it has proved unable to keep pace with a progressive civilization.

- Charles Watts

The object of Christ was to teach his followers how to die, rather than to instruct them how to live. . . . In Spain religion is cruel oppression, in Scotland it is a gloomy nightmare, in Rome it is priestly dominion, while in England it is simply emotional pastime. All these different phases of Christianity indicate that theological opinions depend on surrounding circumstances, and cannot therefore be the cause of the civilization of the world.

- Charles Watts

I also have nothing but contempt for the so-called spiritual leaders who prey upon [religious] people for their own personal financial or political gain.

- Wil Weaton

I'm so fed up with being told that I'm a bad person because I don't subscribe to the same exact narrow views [Christians] have.

- Wil Weaton

As you learn more and more about the universe, you find you can understand more and more without any reference to supernatural intervention, so you lose interest in that possibility. Most scientists I know don't care enough about religion even to call themselves atheists. And that, I think, is one of the greatest things about science—that it has made it possible for people not to be religious.

- Steve Weinberg

The whole history of the last thousands of years has been a history of religious persecutions and wars, pogroms, jihads, crusades. I find it all very regrettable, to say the least.

- Steve Weinberg

Religion is an insult to human dignity. With or without religion, you would have good people doing good things and evil people doing evil things. But for good people to do evil things, that takes religion.

- Steve Weinberg

Debating creationists on the topic of evolution is rather like trying to play chess with a pigeon; it knocks the pieces over, craps on the board, and flies back to its flock to claim victory.

- Scott D. Weitzenhoffer

I say I have no religious beliefs. I certainly think this life is all I have, all anybody has, and I usually say it doesn't seem to at all meaningful to ask the purpose of life. What purpose does the life of a spider have a spider doesn't have a purpose, why should we? Of course, we all have our individual purposes, that's quite different.

- G. A. Wells

Nowadays, you can say practically anything about Jesus without creating offense—so long as you admit he existed. There was no such person.

- G. A. Wells

Indeed Christianity passes. Passes—it has gone! It has littered the beaches of life with churches, cathedrals, shrines and crucifixes, prejudices and intolerances, like the sea urchin and starfish and empty shells and lumps of stinging jelly upon the sands here after a tide. A tidal wave out of Egypt. And it has left a multitude of little wriggling theologians and confessors and apologists hopping and burrowing in the warm nutritious sand. But in the hearts of living men, what remains of it now? Doubtful scraps of Arianism. Phrases. Sentiments. Habits.

- H. G. Wells

Do not any longer contend for mastery, for power, money, or praise. Be content to be a private, insignificant person, known and loved by God and me . . . of what importance is your character to mankind, if you was buried just now. Or if you had never lived, what loss would it be to the cause of God.

- John Wesley

I do not myself find it agreeable to be 90, and I cannot imagine why it should seem so to other people. It is not that you have any fears about your own death, it is that your upholstery is already dead around you.

- Rebecca West

I have no faith in the sense of comforting beliefs which persuade me that all my troubles are blessings in disguise. . . . Creeds pretend to explain the total universe in terms comprehensible to the human intellect, and that pretension seems to me bound to be invalid. . . . The belief that all higher life is governed by the idea of renunciation poisons our moral life. . . . If we do not live for pleasure we will soon find ourselves living for pain.

- Rebecca West

There is one common condition for the lot of women in Western civilization and all other civilizations that we know about for certain, and that is, woman as a sex is disliked and persecuted, while as an individual she is liked, loved, and even, with

196

reasonable luck, sometimes worshiped.

- Rebecca West

Faith in God means believing absolutely in something with no proof whatsoever. Faith in humanity means believing absolutely in something with a huge amount of proof to the contrary. We are the true believers.

- Joss Whedon

[College should be] an asylum for Science—where truth shall be sought for truth's sake, not stretched or cut exactly to fit Revealed Religion.

- Andrew Dickson White

In all modern history, interference with science in the supposed interest of religion, no matter how conscientious such interference may have been, has resulted in the direst evils both to religion and science.

- Andrew Dickson White

I simply try to aid in letting the light of historical truth into that decaying mass of outworn thought which attaches the modern world to medieval conceptions of Christianity.

- Andrew Dickson White

It was a strange little scene. Women were careening about in their cotton print dresses, and several times they nearly threw me off my feet and all but knocked my camera out of my hands as they waved their Bibles and shrieked their 'Praise Be's.'

- Margaret Bourke-White

I think I could turn and live with animals, they're so placid and self contain'd, . . . They do not sweat and whine about their condition, They do not lie awake in the dark and weep for their sins, They do not make me sick discussing their duty to God, Not one is dissatisfied, not one is demented with the mania of owning things, Not one kneels to another, nor to his kind that lived thousands of years ago, Not one is respectable or unhappy over the earth.

- Walt Whitman

This is what you shall do: Love the earth and sun and animals, despise riches, give alms to everyone that asks, stand up for the stupid and crazy, devote your income and labor to others, hate tyrants, argue not concerning God.

- Walt Whitman

So many Gods, so many creeds, so many paths that wind and wind, when just the art of being kind is all this sad world needs.

- Ella Wheeler Wilcox

A thing is not necessarily true because a man dies for it.

- Oscar Wilde

I think that God in creating Man somewhat overestimated his ability.

- Oscar Wilde

It is better for the artist not to live with popes

- Oscar Wilde

Science is the record of dead religions.

- Oscar Wilde

The only way to get rid of a temptation is to yield to it.

- Oscar Wilde

There is no sin except stupidity.

- Oscar Wilde

Truth, in matters of religion, is simply the opinion that has survived.

- Oscar Wilde

The marks of philosophy are reflection and heightened self-awareness, not maximal transcendence of the human perspective. . . . There is no cosmic point of view, and therefore no test of cosmic significance.

- Bernard Williams

There is no reason why an atheist could not write a good Mass.

- Ralph Vaughan Williams

God requireth not an uniformity of Religion to be inacted and inforced in any civil state.

- Roger Williams

[Ralph Vaughan Williams] was an atheist during his later years at Charterhouse and at Cambridge, though he later drifted into a cheerful agnosticism: he was never a professing Christian.

- Ursula Vaughan Williams

Organized religions in general, in my opinion, are dying forms. They were all very important when we didn't know why the sun moved, why weather changed, why hurricanes occurred, or volcanoes happened. Modern religion is the end trail of modern mythology. But there are people who interpret the Bible literally. Literally! I choose not to believe that's the way. And that's what makes America cool, you know?

- Bruce Willis

If someone could actually prove scientifically that there is such a thing as a supernatural force, it would be one of the greatest discoveries in the history of science. So the notion that somehow scientists are resisting it is ludicrous.

- E. O. Wilson

It is essential to understand that *true* freedom of Religion must include freedom *from* Religion.

- Paul Winchell

It is my contention that no other invention of man has brought greater chaos to humanity than the practice of religion.

- Paul Winchell

If I were a CEO of a company and ran it like God runs the universe, I'd be fired.

- Sherwin Wine

Belief is an anomaly of the mind.

- Ben Winter

It is a strange religion. A strange religion, indeed.

- P. G. Wodehouse

I am committed to science and believe it to be the best way to understand the world . . . I know of no good evidence for the existence of God.

- Lewis Wolpert

I was quite a religious child, saying my prayers each night and asking God for help on various occasions. It did not seem to help and I gave it all up around 16 and have been an atheist ever since.

- Lewis Wolpert

Once you had that concept which enabled you to manufacture complex tools, you then wanted to understand other things as well—why we got ill, what happened when we died, why the sun shone or disappeared. Those, too, must have causes. And that's the origin of belief.

- Lewis Wolpert

No legal ceremony—no election of the woman—no penalty for the perfidy of the man—no law to compel him to do his duty, no compensation for the poor woman who is turned adrift like the girl of the street, penniless, to sell herself on the best possible terms. This is Divine marriage, or Moses and the Bible lie; and this is Bible divorce—putting away!

- Victoria Woodhull

200

I read the Book of Job last night—I don't think God comes well out of it.

- Virginia Woolf

I just felt that an intelligent person like myself could figure out good behaviors without going to a church and having to follow the thinking of a large group, all who follow it largely because they all do.

- Steve Wozniak

I've never been to church and prefer to think for myself.

- Steve Wozniak

I am not going to question your opinions. I am not going to meddle with your belief. I am not going to dictate to you mine. All that I say is, examine, inquire. Look into the nature of things. Search out the grounds of your opinions, the for and the against. Know why you believe, understand what you believe, and possess a reason for the faith that is in you.

- Frances Wright

Turn your churches into halls of science, and devote your leisure day to the study of your own bodies, the analysis of your own minds, and the examination of the material world which extends around you!

- Frances Wright

I believe in God, only I spell it Nature.

- Frank Lloyd Wright

I have no religion in the formal sense of the word. . . . I have no race except that which is forced upon me. I have no country except that to which I'm obliged to belong. I have no traditions. I'm free. I have only the future.

- Richard Wright

# YOUNG

The only men who become Gods, even the sons of God, are those who enter into polygamy.

- Brigham Young

# ZAPPA

Anybody who wants religion is welcome to it, as far as I'm concerned—I support your right to enjoy it. However, I would appreciate it if you exhibited more respect for the rights of those people who do not wish to share your dogma, rapture, or necrodestination.

- Frank Zappa

I did have a strong Catholic background, but I am not a Catholic. Somewhere in the past, I believe I answered in the affirmative once for strange and complicated reasons. But I am not a member of any organized religion. If you mention my Catholic background, I hope you also mention that I became a retired Catholic at age 16. I do not consider myself a Christian.

- Roger Zelazny

If I was promised that we could sit with Marx in some great Deli Haus in the hereafter, I might believe in it! Sure, I find inspiration in Jewish stories of hope, also in the Christian pacifism of the Berrigans, also in Taoism and Buddhism. I identify as a Jew, but not on religious grounds. Yes, I believe, as Pascal said, 'The heart has its reasons which reason cannot know.' There are limits to reason. There is mystery, there is passion, there is something spiritual in the arts—but it is not connected to Judaism or any other religion.

- Howard Zinn

Willful Ignorance is both a life and death sentence.

- James A. Zoppa

I think Facebook might be the first place where a large number of people have come out. . . . We didn't create that—society was generally ready for that.

- Mark Zuckerberg

## About the Author:

Originally from Chicago, Steve Dustcircle comes from a background in religious ministry and music performance, but now has his hand in many forms of activism, mostly focused on free thought and human rights. There is not much he hasn't done; there is little that he hasn't read about. Steve lives in Columbus, OH with his frugal-blogger wife, and loves good coffee, cold lager, and stimulating conversation.

Steve authored and edited several short books:

*Politics for the Disinterested*

*Mangasarian Volume 1*

*Transport* (a novella)

*Napkins* (poetry & short stories)

*Unchristianed Nation*

*The Quotable Dissenting Heretic*

and *Before Your First Gig.*

All can be purchased from aLife Beyond Books.

Printed in Great Britain
by Amazon